ITTY BITTY ANIMALS

Stories from the Rehabilitation Center

Goats, Cows, Rabbits, Horses

by Susan Weimer

Copyright: November 2017

Table of Contents

Goats
Billy 2
Rendezvous 4
Clyde 6
Elvis 8
Alcott 10
Nibblet 12
Altai 14
Scape 16
Elvira 18
Marbles 20

Cows
Caroline 24
Pontchartrain 26
Gemini 28
Mercedes 30
Wellington 32
Strawberry 34
Grape Juice 36
Diamond 38

Table of Contents

Rabbits

Meringue..............................42

Patton 44

Bugs 46

Cleopatra 48

Ginger.................................50

Savoy 52

Lime-a-Rita 54

Velveteen 56

Clover 58

Fluffy 60

Horses

Old Paint.............................64

Knight's Mare.....................66

Bean 68

Lightning 70

Widow Maker 72

Credit Card.........................74

Old Master..........................76

Billie Jean 78

This book is dedicated to

C W Sparrow

who

washes and folds the laundry

washes and dries the dishes

washes the Kia Soul

sweeps the floor

fills the humidifier

puts gas in the Kia Soul

takes out the trash

cleans the kitty litter box

feeds the fish

feeds the birds

GOATS

Billy was found in Minnesota checking out bridges for trolls. We had to explain to him that there were no trolls. But his experience with bridges made him an excellent candidate to work for the US Department of Transportation as a bridge inspector throughout the United States. Billy is a very intelligent goat and with encouragement earned his degree in civil engineering. He is delightfully entertaining with all of his "bridge" experiences and stories. He needs a good stable family life and would love to go home with you.

Billy

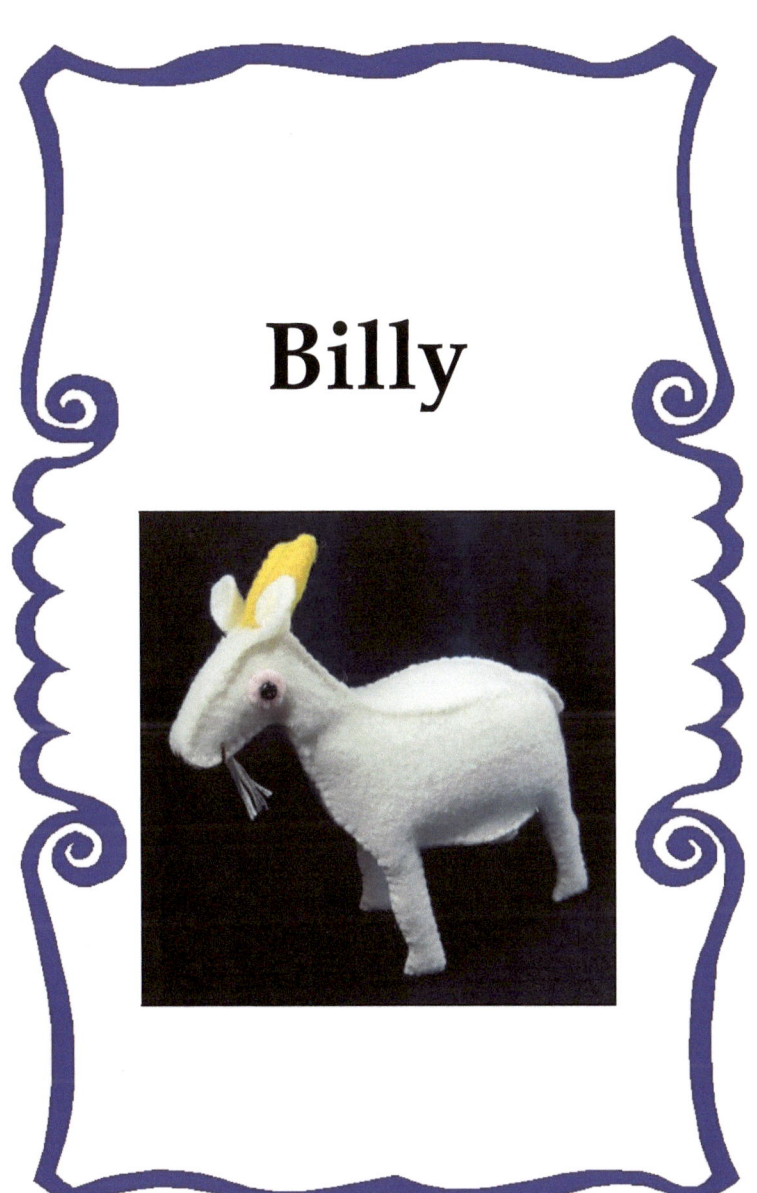

Rendezvous is a mythical goat. He was found in Never-Never Land in the galley of a ship peeling potatoes. He was befriended by Peter Pan and rescued from the dreadful conditions of the galley. After his rehabilitation period, Rendezvous was trained in the ancient art of head butting pirates off of ships. He went from a potato peeler to a fearless and dedicated "pirate butt-er." Do you need a confident pet in your life? Do you need a goat who understands your love of fantasy and make-believe? Then Rendezvous is the goat for you.

Rendezvous

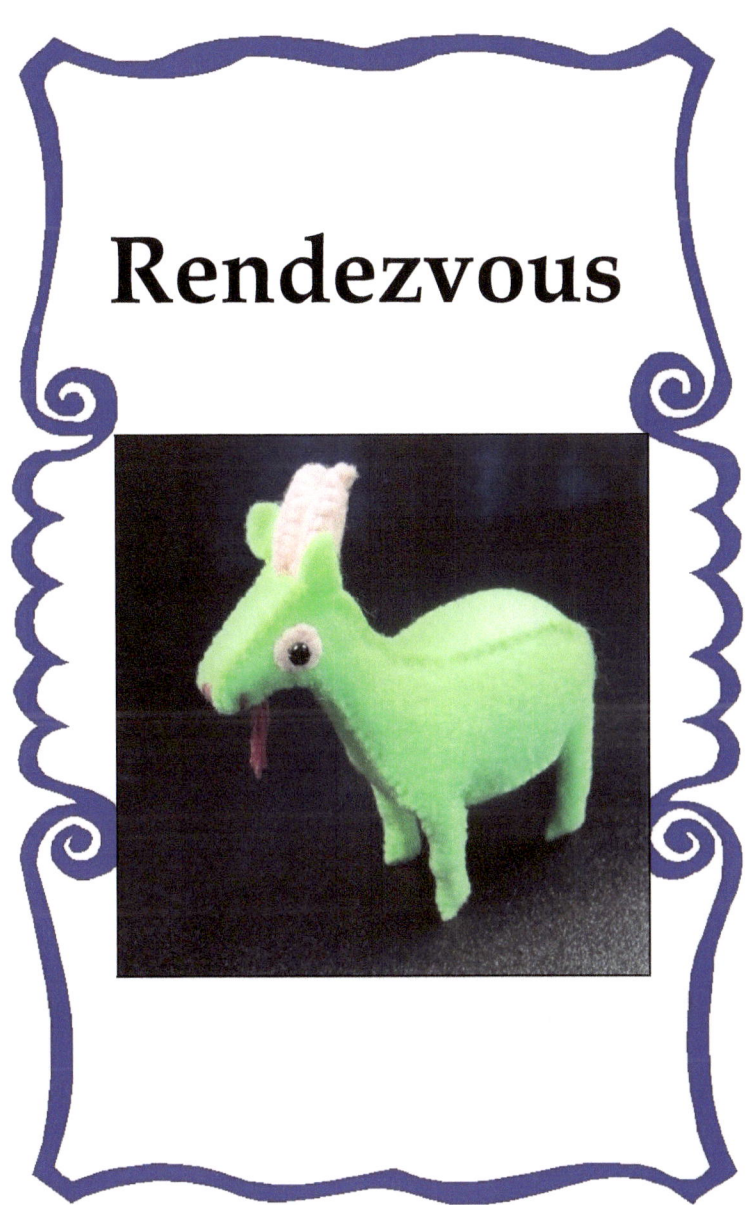

Clyde is a very unique goat. He was found in Michigan eating the sheets off of a clothesline. He said he wanted to become a "stuffed goat." After his rehabilitation period, our crew found out that he is an excellent trail navigator. We trained him to lead hikes and he is now an expert trail blazer. You will not get lost when Clyde is in control. He is a natural born leader and is an avid outdoor goat. Clyde's love of the outdoors has fed a desire to be a ski instructor. Do you love skiing? Then Clyde is the perfect companion for you. He needs a loving home. Could that home be yours?

Clyde

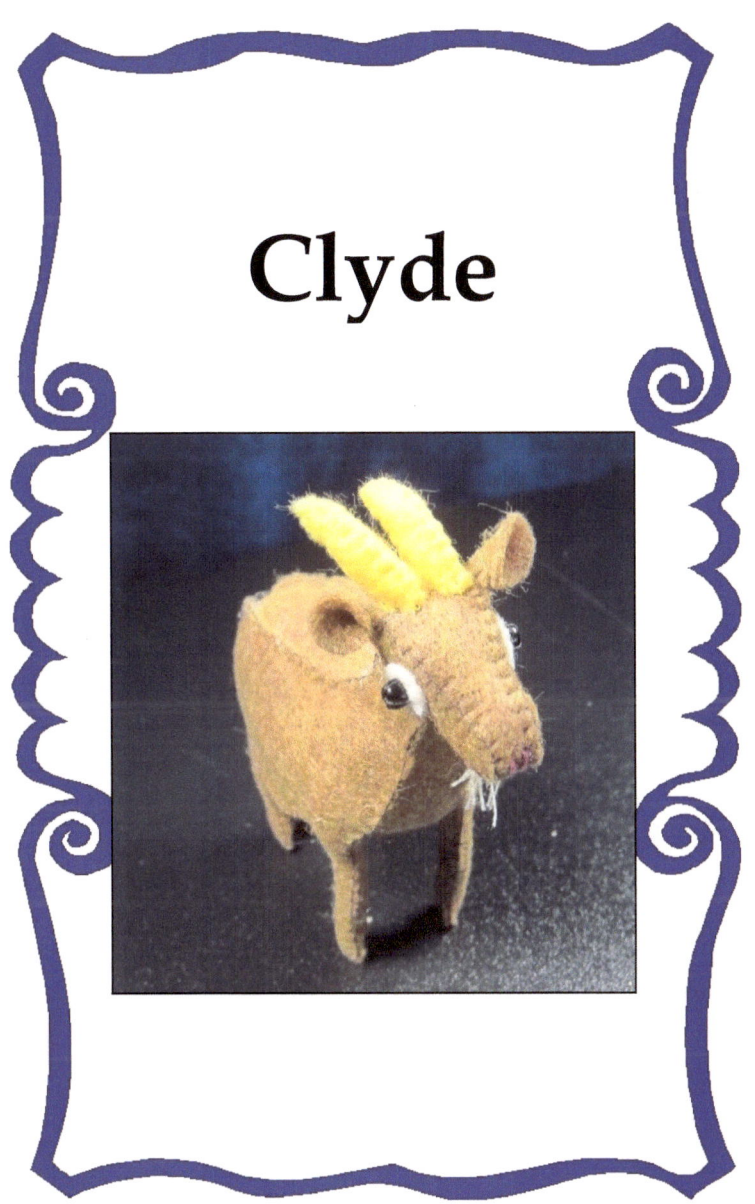

Elvis was found on a street corner in Memphis, Tennessee playing the blues on his guitar. The Grand Ole Opry snatched him up and he got his start in the music industry. He expanded his blues repertoire to include rock and roll. He does not let fame go to his head; Elvis is a very humble goat. He would make a great companion for a music lover. His work is eclectic and he loves experimenting with new forms and types of music. Are you a music lover? Are you willing to encourage Elvis as he pursues his musical career? If so, Elvis is the goat for you.

Elvis

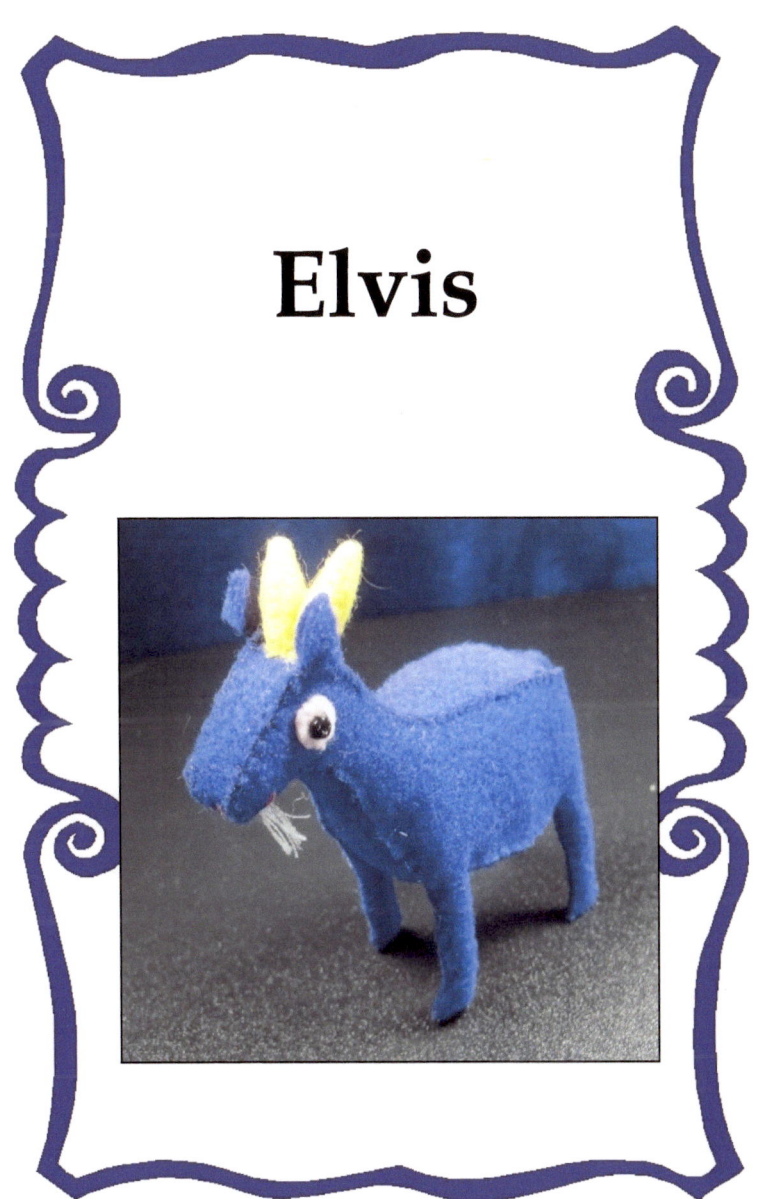

Alcott was rescued from a petting zoo near Boston, Massachusetts. She loves being with people, especially children. Alcott's interests center around reading and writing. She is working on a non-fiction book which is titled, *How to Get Your Goat*. She loves eating out and is fond of pizza and Mexican food. Alcott has had all her shots and is housebroken. She would make a wonderful pet for someone who is affectionate, loving, and welcoming. She needs help with the book she is writing. Could that special someone be you?

Alcott

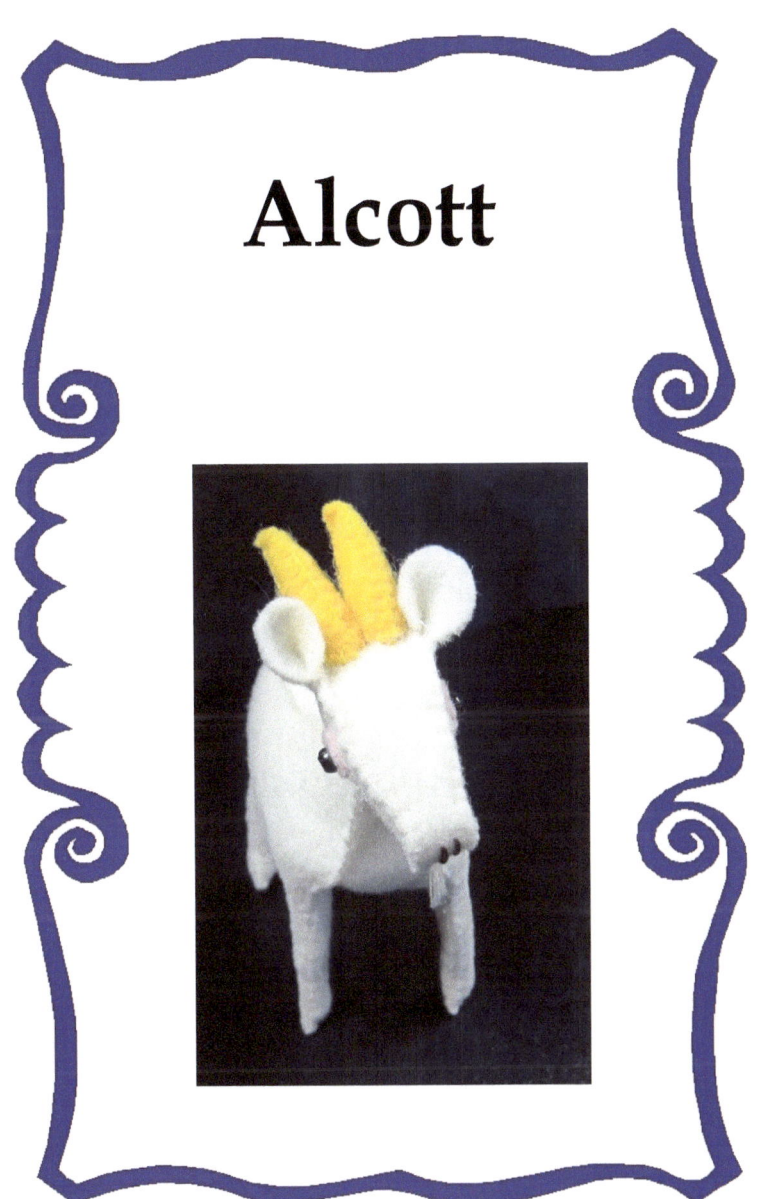

This is Nibblet. He is a vegetable taste tester for the Jolly Purple Giant in Montana. Nibblet is quite a unique goat. His specialty is eating corn and producing a gas that can be used in lawnmowers and ATV's. His gas is manufactured in a secret shed where no one will be offended by the ghastly smell of the product he produces. Once it is contained, the gas is ready to be used. Although Nibblet can be a rather smelly goat, the problem is nothing a little goat cologne can't solve. Are you willing to work with his unusual gifts? He needs a loving and kind home life that will make him feel welcome.

Nibblet

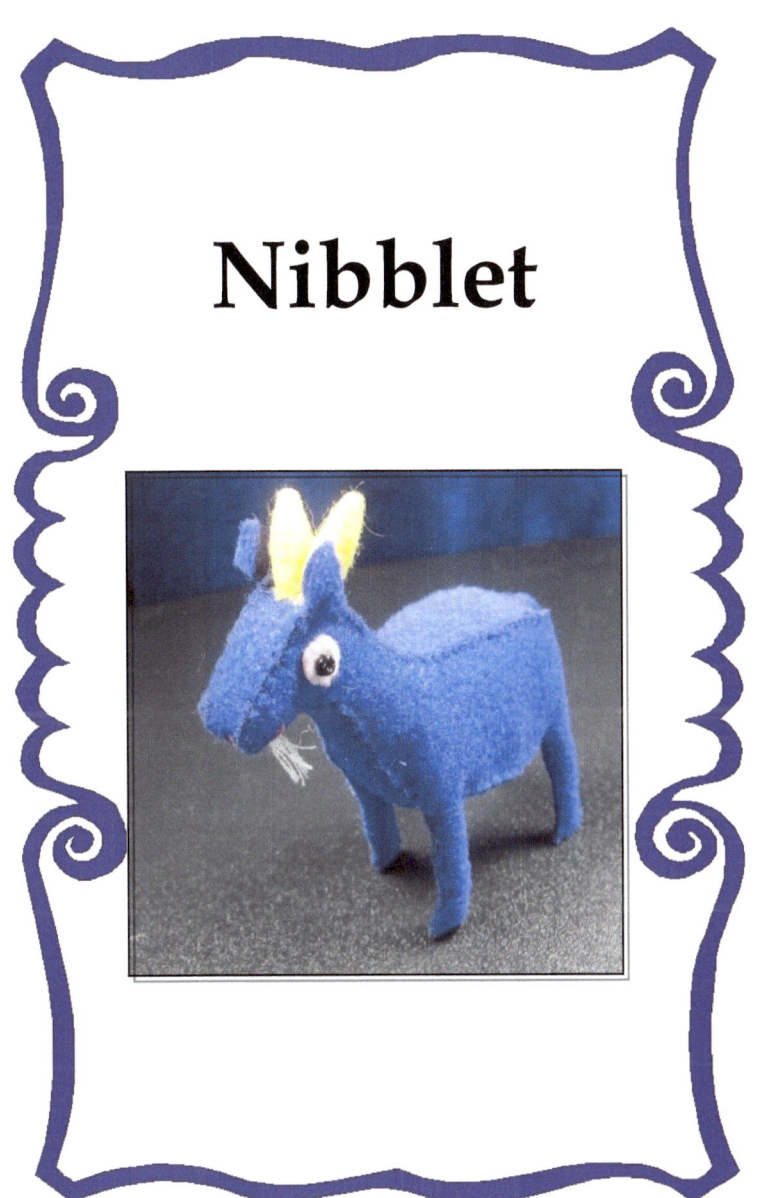

Altai is a shaman. She understands the environmental concerns of the indigenous people scattered throughout the world. Her native country, Altai, is losing its glaciers at an alarming pace. She touches the spirits of her native land and ancestors and continues to seek healing for her land and people. She does not want to lose the ancient traditions of her people and holds her post in high regard. She relates well to conservationists and the harmony brought about by respect for nature, land, natural resources, lakes and rivers, and the oceans. Altai is a very special goat but is not domineering. Is she the right pet for you?

Altai

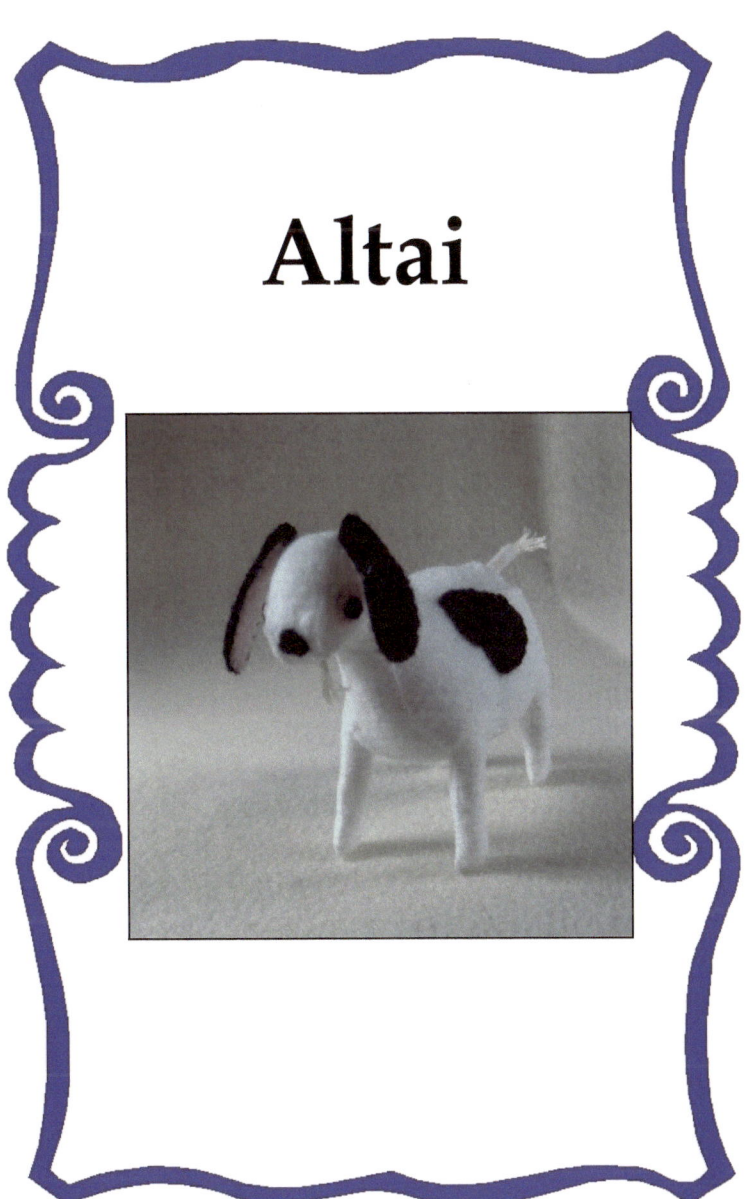

Scape was found working in a salt mine in southern Israel. He was tired, hungry, and very sad. He said that he felt like he was carrying the weight of the world on his back. Our rescue crew brought him to our rehab compound in Israel. He has been housebroken and has all his shs. Scape is a very sentimental goat and strives to help humanity overcome its prejudices and distrust of one another. But he is also a shrewd diplomat and is looking to become the Ambassador to the Middle East and Israel. Can you support Scape in this incredible mission?

Scape

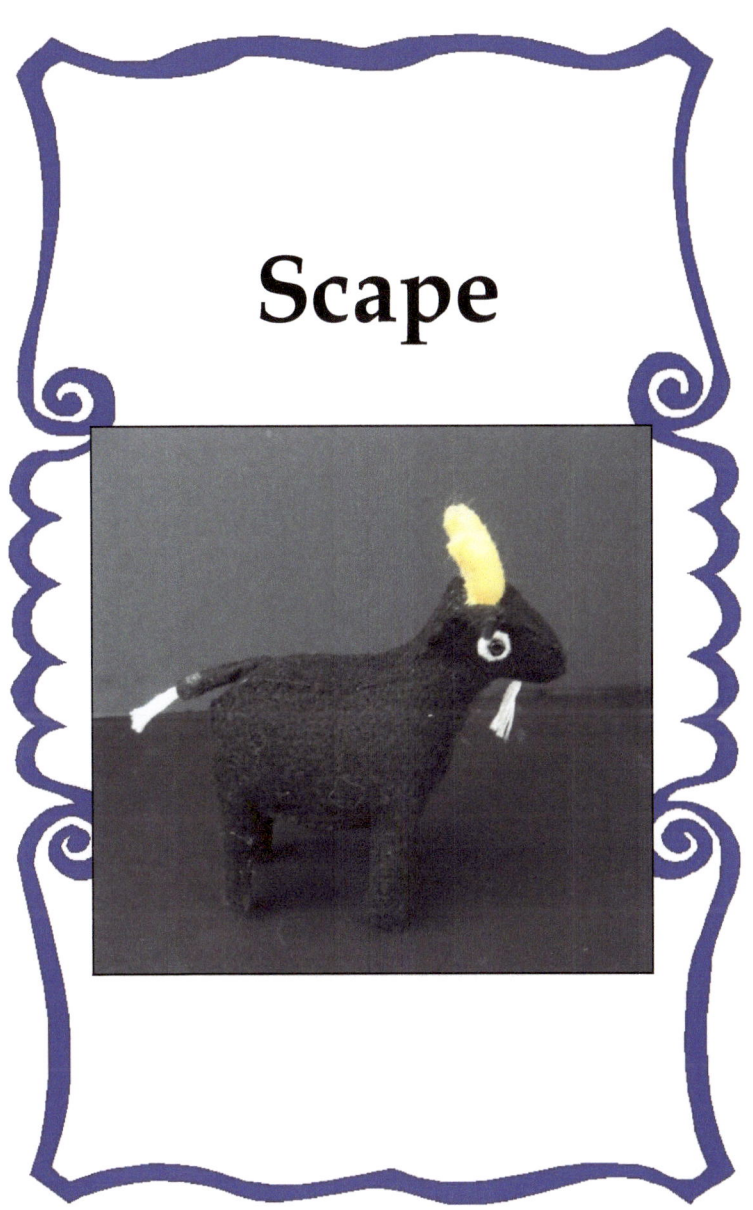

This is Elvira. Elvira is the Addams' family pet goat. She eats almost anything and in particular she loves to eat computers. She is very unique because she has a hidden antenna in each of her horns. With these antennae, she can locate a hacker within a 500 mile radius. When she locates a hacker, she goes to that location and eats the hacker's computer! She has been sought after by Target, Home Depot, and the Federal Government, but she prefers going home with a loving and kind person. Are you the right person for Elvira?

Elvira

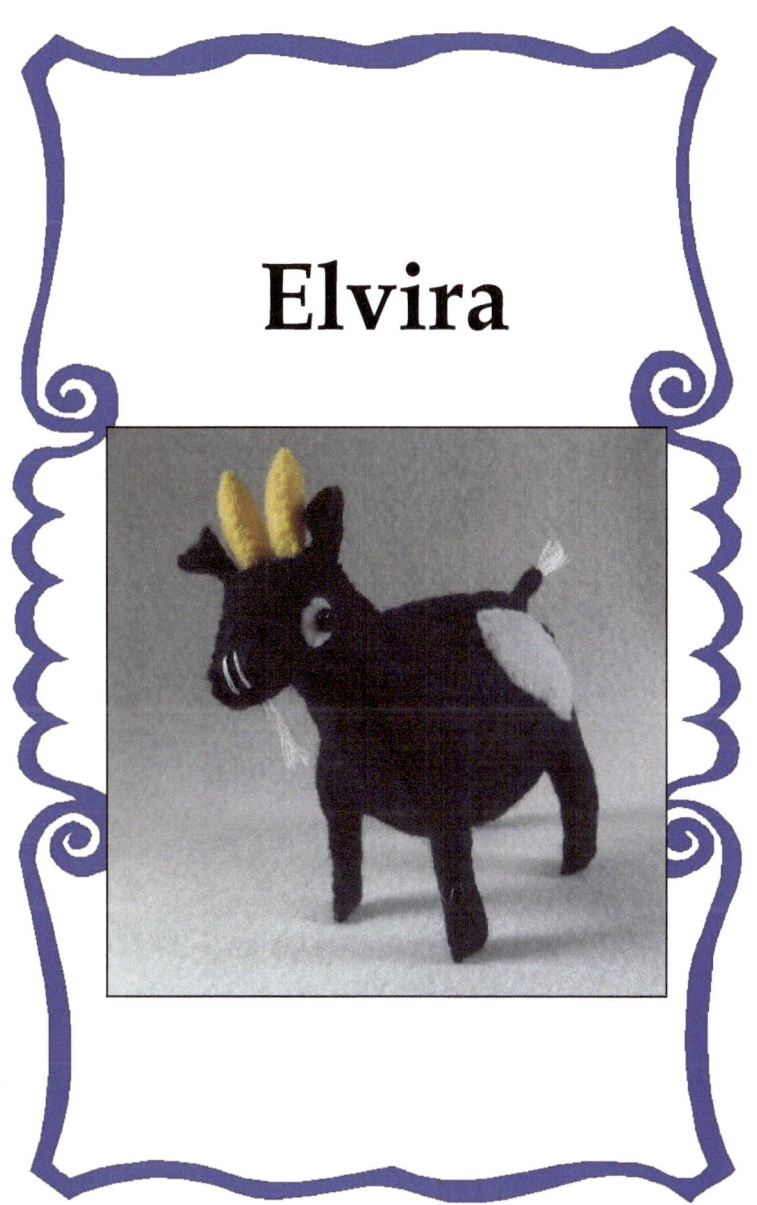

Marbles was rescued from a Biloxi, Mississippi jail. He was a caught in a raid which broke up the intense "winner-take-all" marbles game. He was about to lose all his marbles when he was picked up. Our rescue team was called to take him to our rehabilitation center. He came with only two marbles. The team recognized his skills at shooting marbles and trimmed his hooves for a chance at perfecting his shots. He has moved up the marble championship event calendar, and he shows great promise. Are you willing to help Marbles achieve his goal? He just might bring home a marble championship trophy!

Marbles

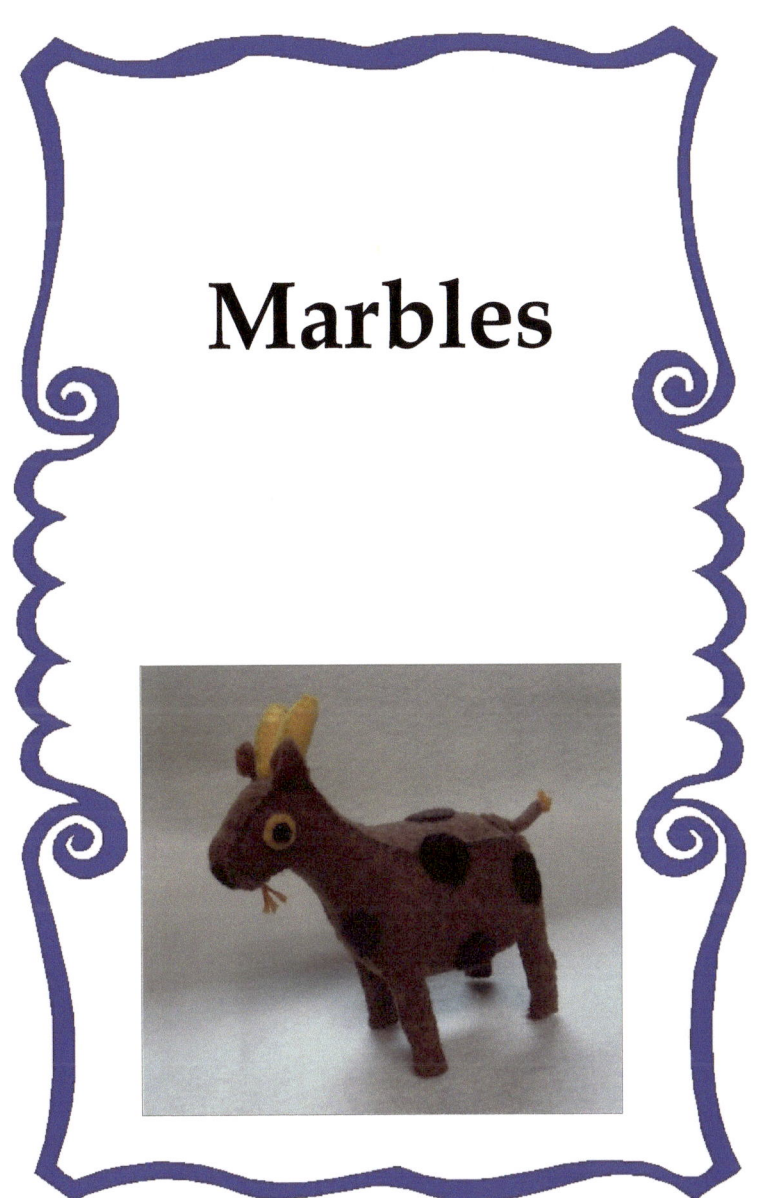

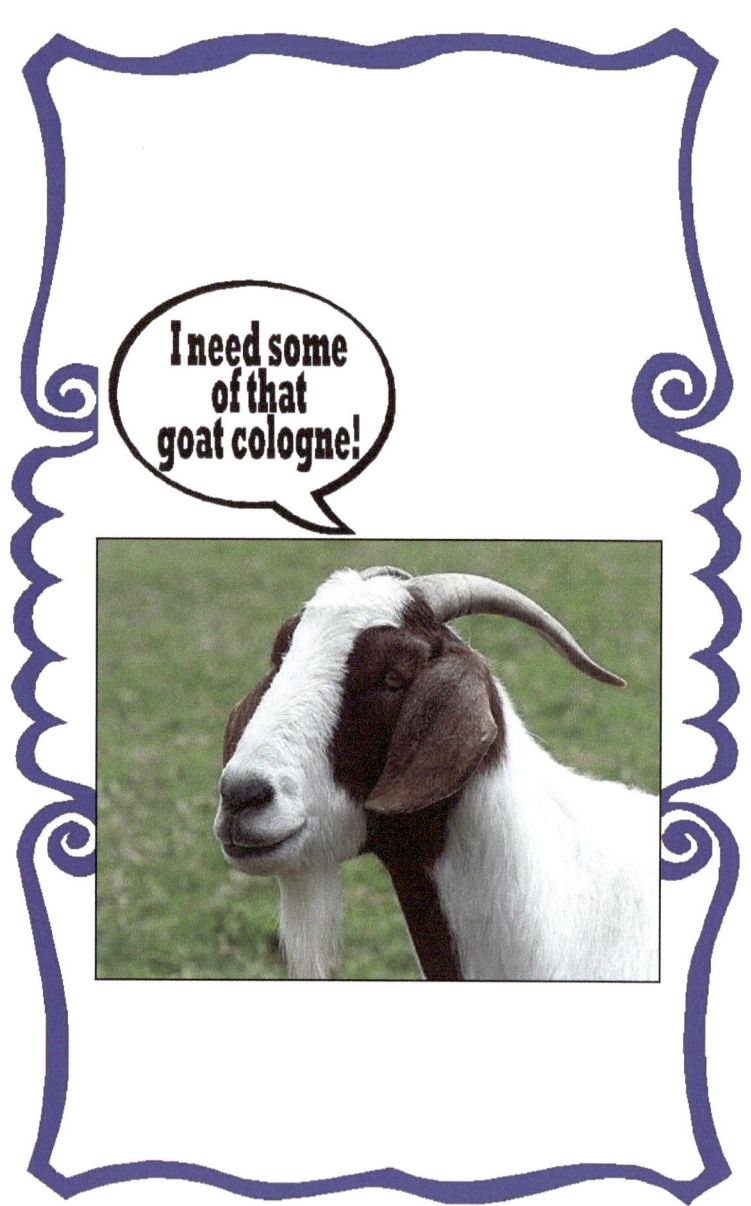

COWS

Caroline is a sweet, good natured calf in need of a loving home. She was born and bred in North Carolina and was abandoned when her farm was closed down. She has all her shots, is housebroken, and has a microchip in case she gets lost. She loves to be read to and enjoys all types of farm stories. She does well in school and is hoping to go to college. She has an endowment so is well taken care of. Caroline needs you in her life!

Caroline

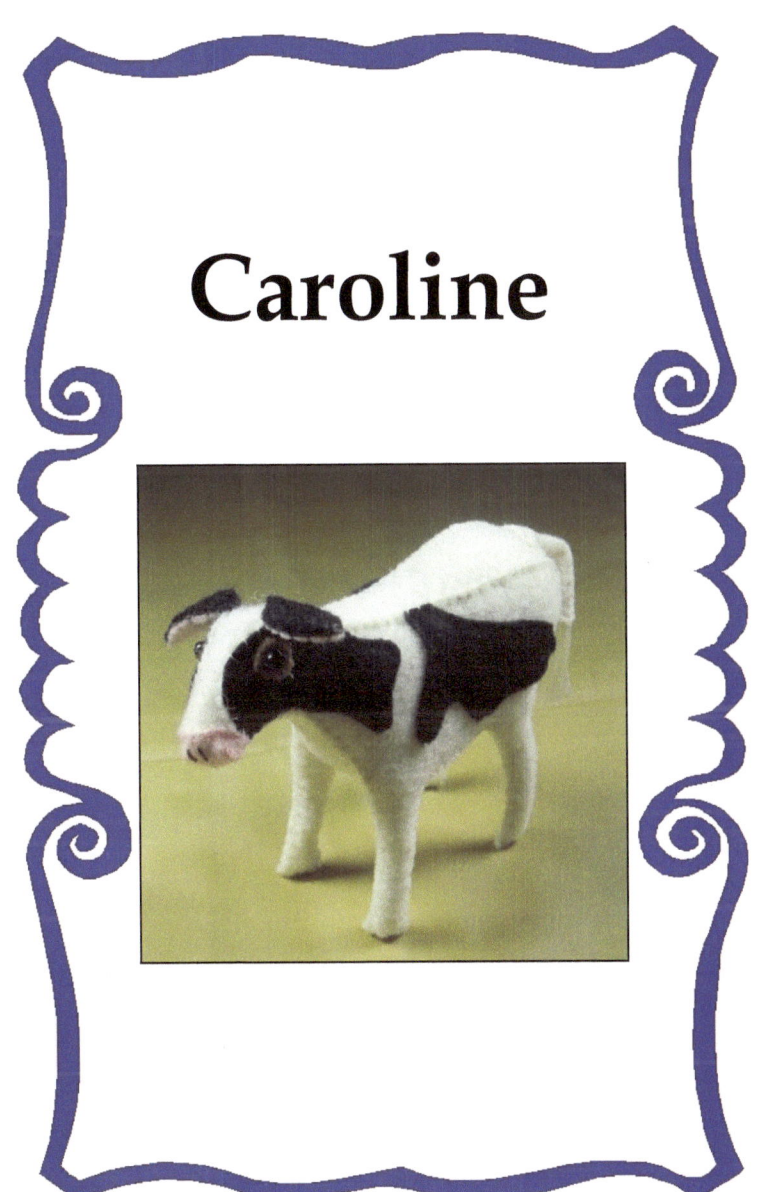

Pontchartrain was found in the ninth ward of New Orleans shortly after Hurricane Katrina. FEMA found him a nice trailer but he had trouble finding work. He is a kind and loving calf and responds well to meaningful petting. He loves chicken sandwiches, pizza, and barbeque. Pontchartrain is good with children, tolerates dogs and cats and is in need of a loving home. You could not find a better pet. Is he right for you?

Pontchartrain

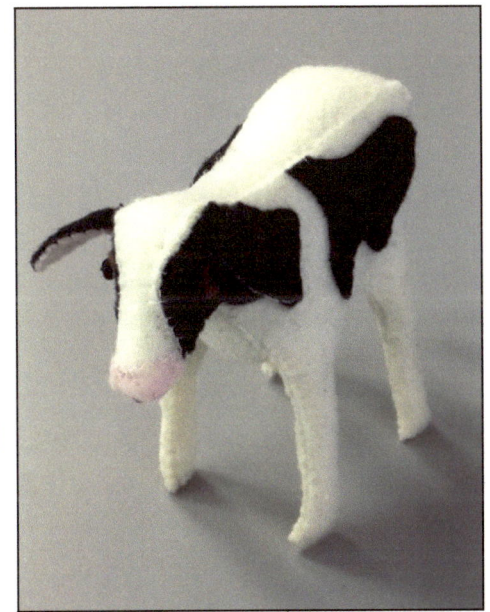

Gemini was found wandering a back road in New Hampshire. He said he was heading south because he wanted to attend astronaut school. His life's ambition is to be one of the cows that "jumped over the moon." He is a very determined and focused calf. Although his interests revolve around the planetary system, he is also interested in world affairs. Our crew gave Gemini all his shots and house-trained him. If you are interested in helping Gemini realize his life dream, then he is the perfect pet for you. How many people have a pet with the aspiration of jumping over the moon?

Gemini

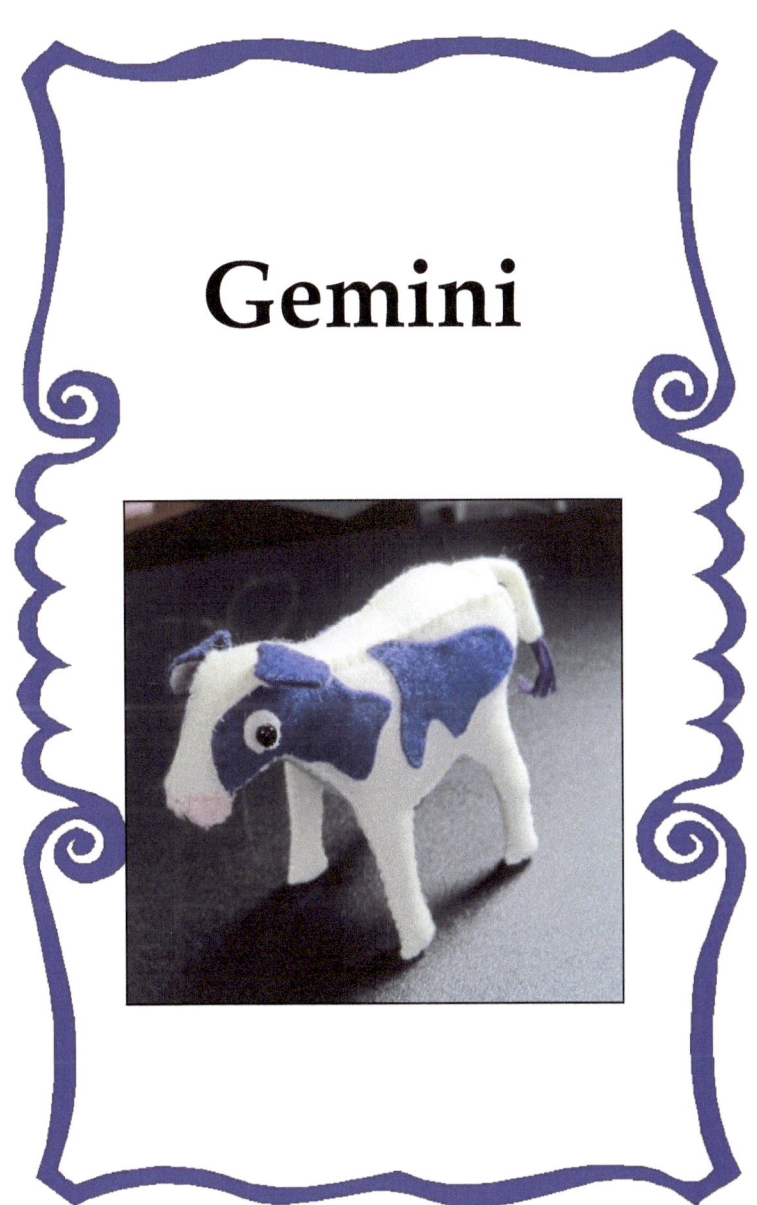

Mercedes was discovered on a golf course in Merced County, California. She was collecting and selling golf balls to make a living. She loves golf and would make a great golfing buddy. She can easily carry your golf clubs, fetch balls, and she can even drive a golf cart! Mercedes is a very encouraging cow on the golf course. She can be trusted with not divulging your golf score unless you are happy with your score. Do you need that perfect golfing buddy? Then Mercedes is the pet for you.

Mercedes

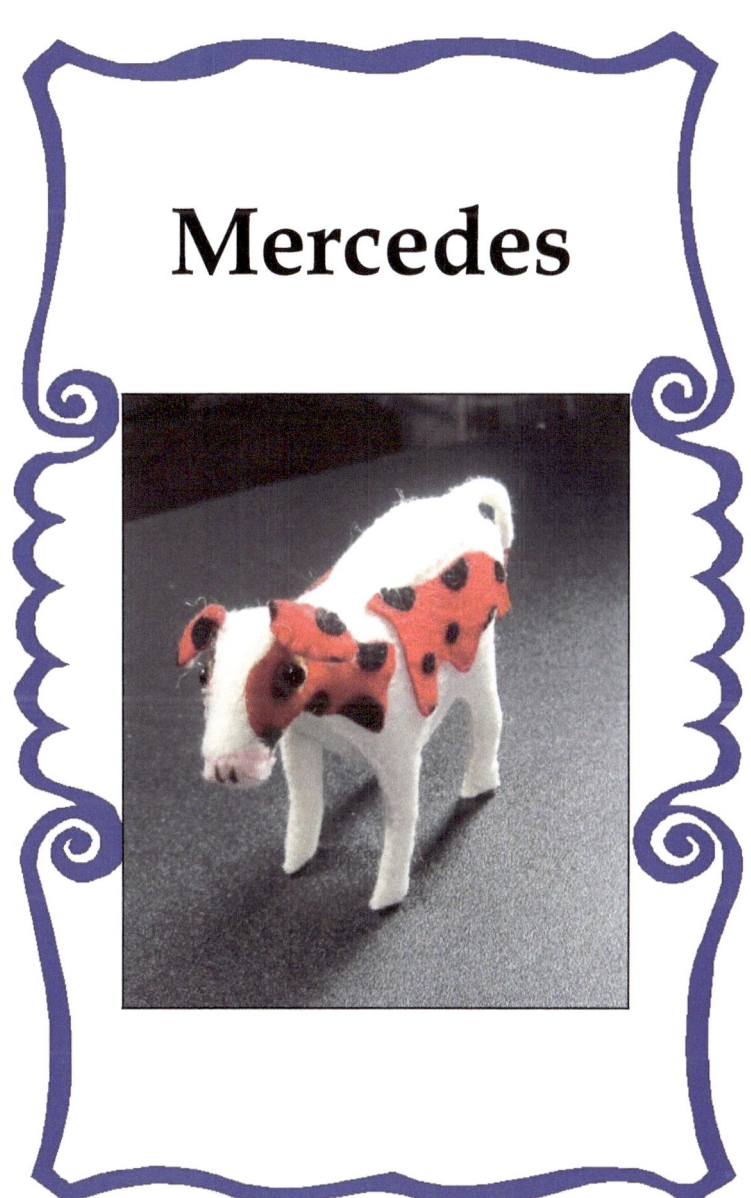

Wellington was discovered on a subway in downtown Manhattan. He was running away from country life and was headed for Wall Street because he wanted to become a "bull." He is good with numbers and wants to become a stock broker. He has had all his shots and is housebroken. He has not been neutered because of his aspirations for "bullhood." Wellington is a great conversationalist and would make a good companion for a person interested in a financial career. Are you the right person for Wellington?

Wellington

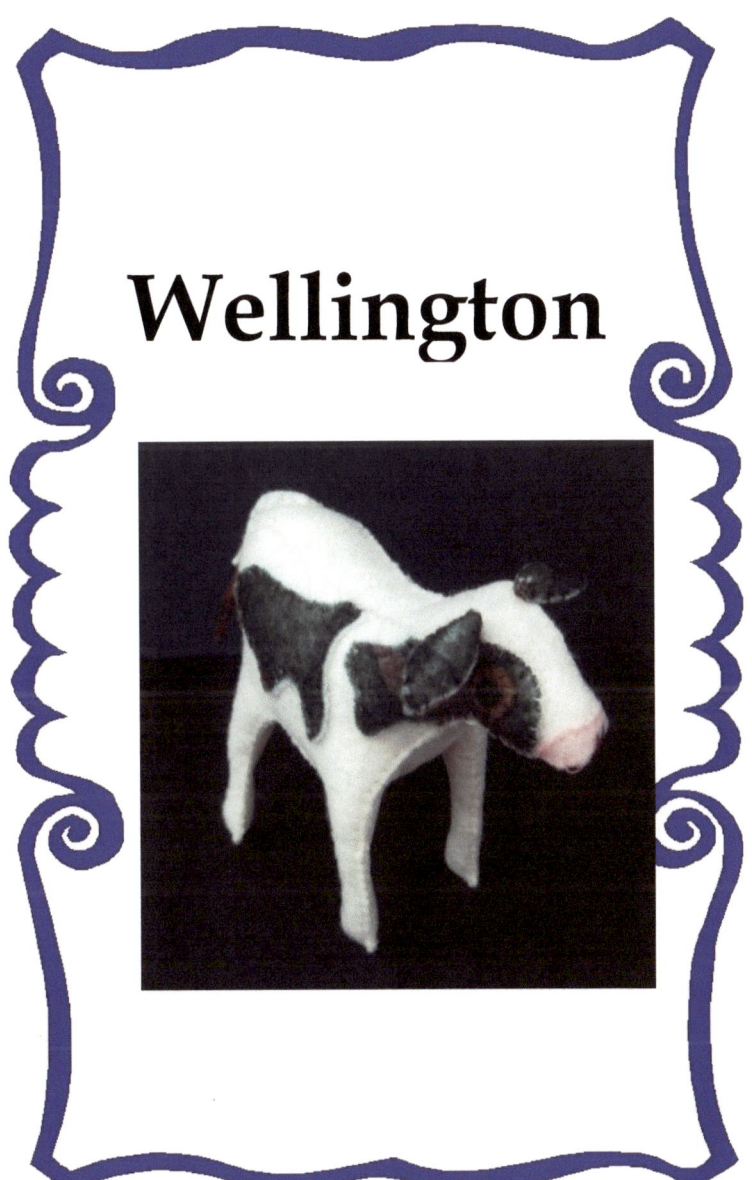

Strawberry raises strawberries, eats them, and makes strawberry shakes. Her distinctly pink milk has that special strawberry flavor that makes her shakes so sought after. She is thinking of expanding her business to include strawberry cream pies, strawberry milk pops, strawberry ice cream, strawberry cow cakes, and a host of other products. She maintains a small shop in downtown New York City near Times Square. You can tell where her shop is because of all the cows outside. If you love strawberries, milk, and cows, then Strawberry is the pet for you.

Strawberry

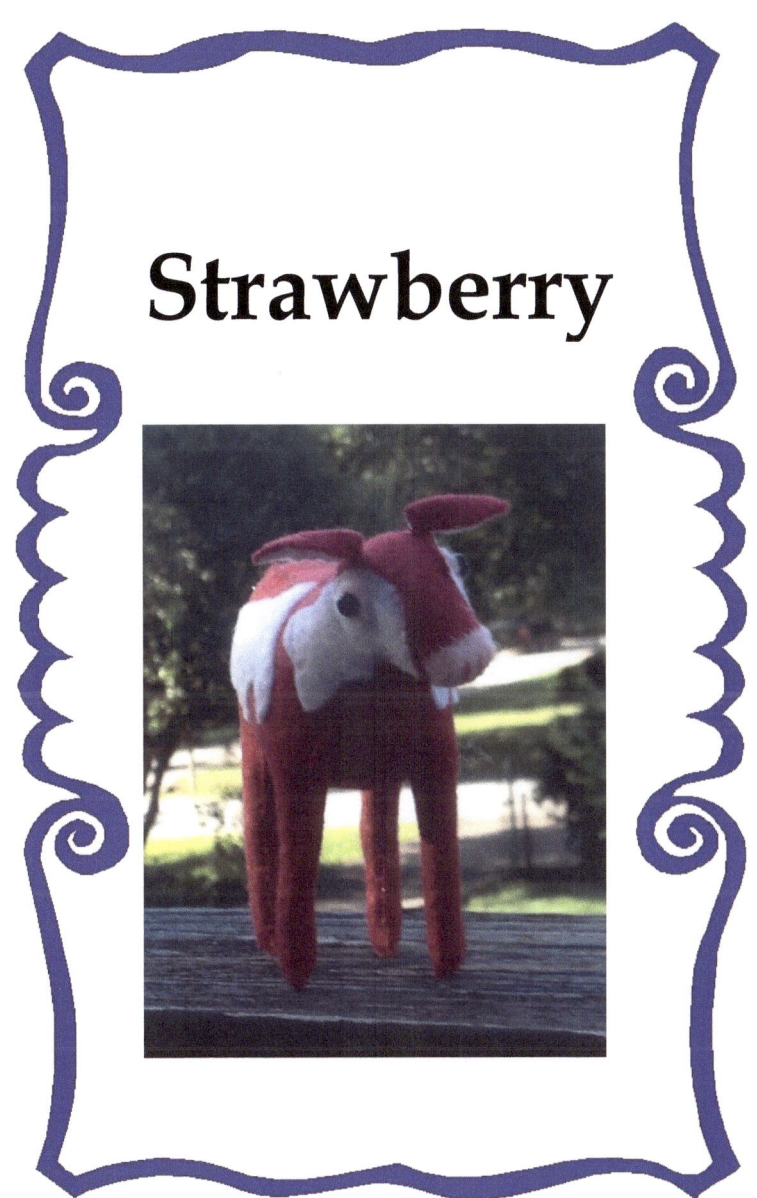

I never saw a purple cow,

I hope to never see one,

But I can tell you, anyhow,

I'd rather see one than be one!

                Gilett Burgess 1895

Grape Juice

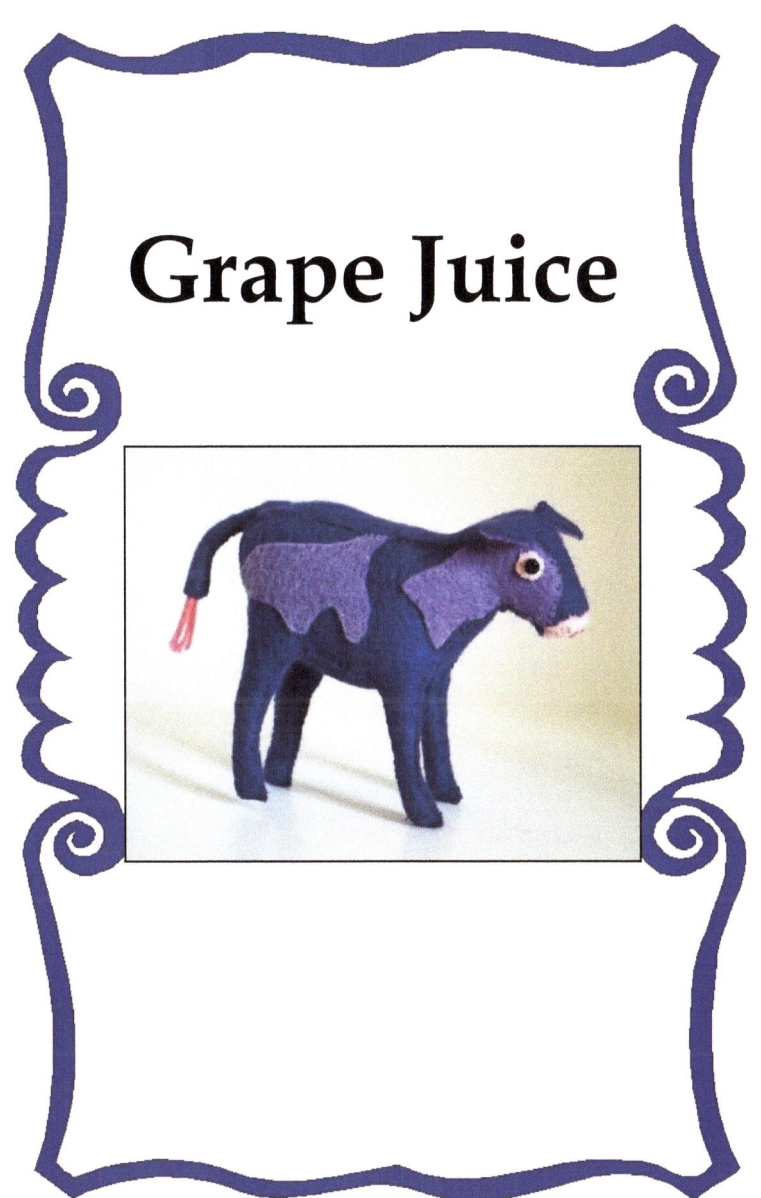

Diamond is a girl's best friend. Your girl will cherish her Diamond forever and she will be convinced of your true love for her. Girls love diamonds, luxury cars, and a big fat checking account. But diamonds are their first love. Diamond will test the love of your girl-friend, wife, or significant other because she will fall in love with it and won't want to put her hands in the dish pan. Your girl will eventually get over that. Diamond is housetrained and has a microchip. Diamond needs a forever home. Do you have that special girl that you need to spoil? Then Diamond is the pet for you!

Diamond

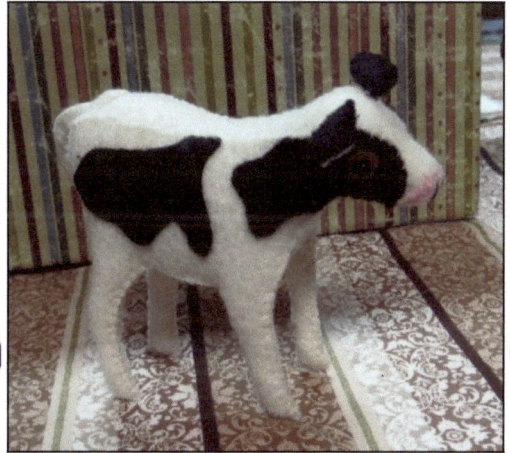

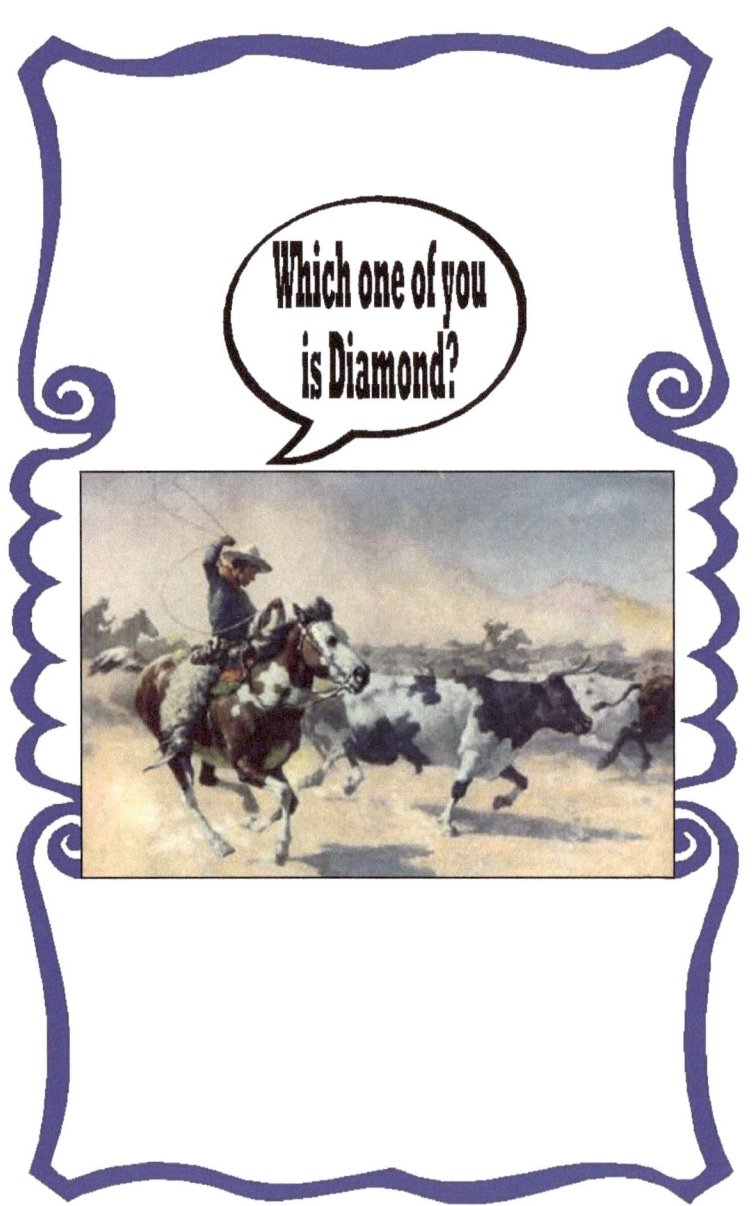

RABBITS

This is Meringue. She was rescued from a bakery hiding under a shelf of lemon meringue pies. She is looking for a kind and loving home. Meringue loves to sample baked goods and is fond of home cooking. She has been spayed, has all her shots, has been housebroken, and has an implanted microchip. She is most proud of her little green tail! Are you the right person for Meringue?

Meringue

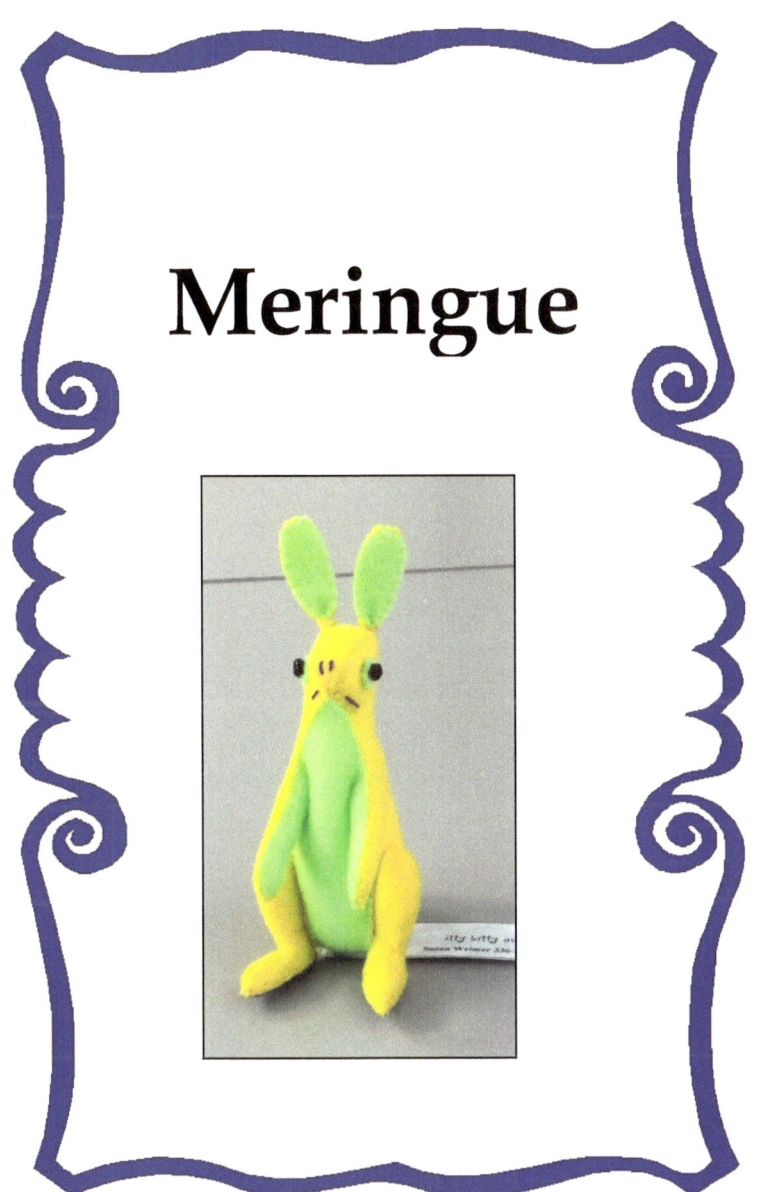

Patton is a very protective rabbit. He has been raised in a military family and was found wandering around an army base. He is well-disciplined but also kind and gentle. His military training gives him the background to replace your home security system. He loves to study military history and is hoping for an appointment to West Point. He has had all his shots; he is neutered; he is housebroken and has a microchip. He loves to snuggle and makes a great sleeping companion. Is Patton right for you? Are you willing to help him reach his dreams? Take Patton home with you today!

Patton

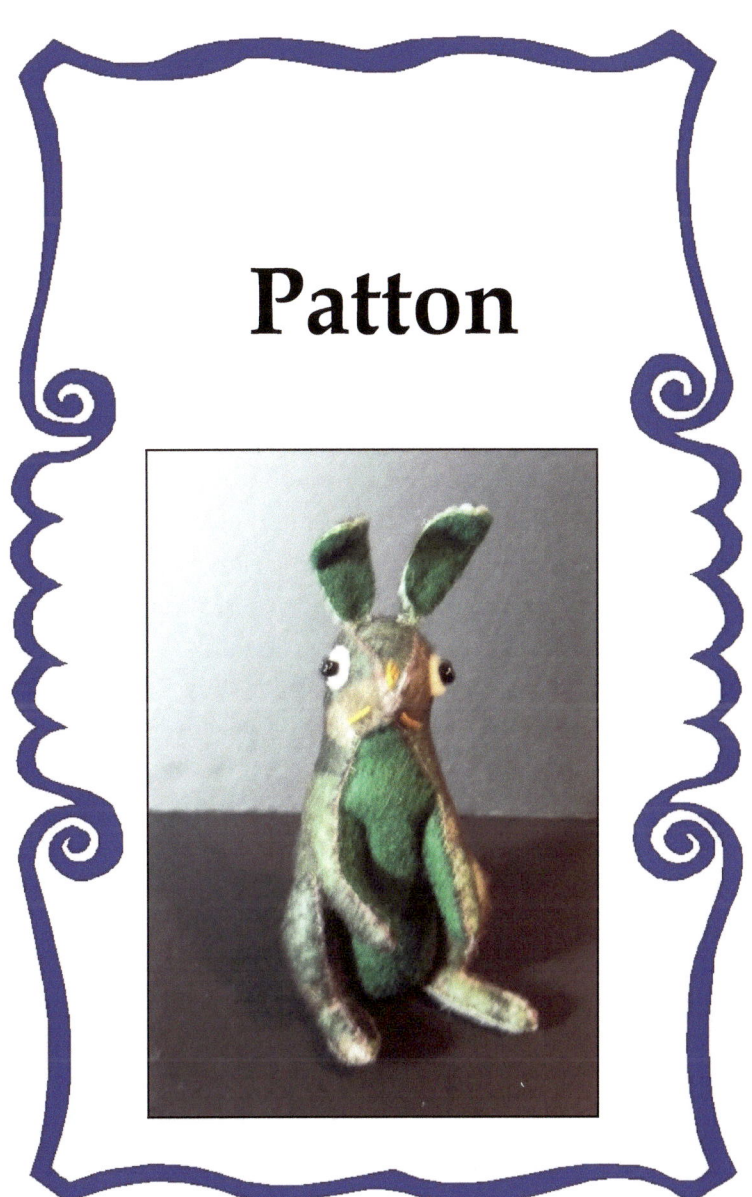

Bugs was spotted wandering the grounds of Disneyland in Florida. He loves the Disney movies and has a gentle and loving nature. He loves pizza, corn dogs, and lettuce. He has all his shots, has been neutered, is housebroken, and has a microchip. He is an indoor rabbit and prefers staying in movie theaters. Bugs can be very entertaining and has had some acting experience. Is Bugs the pet for you?

Bugs

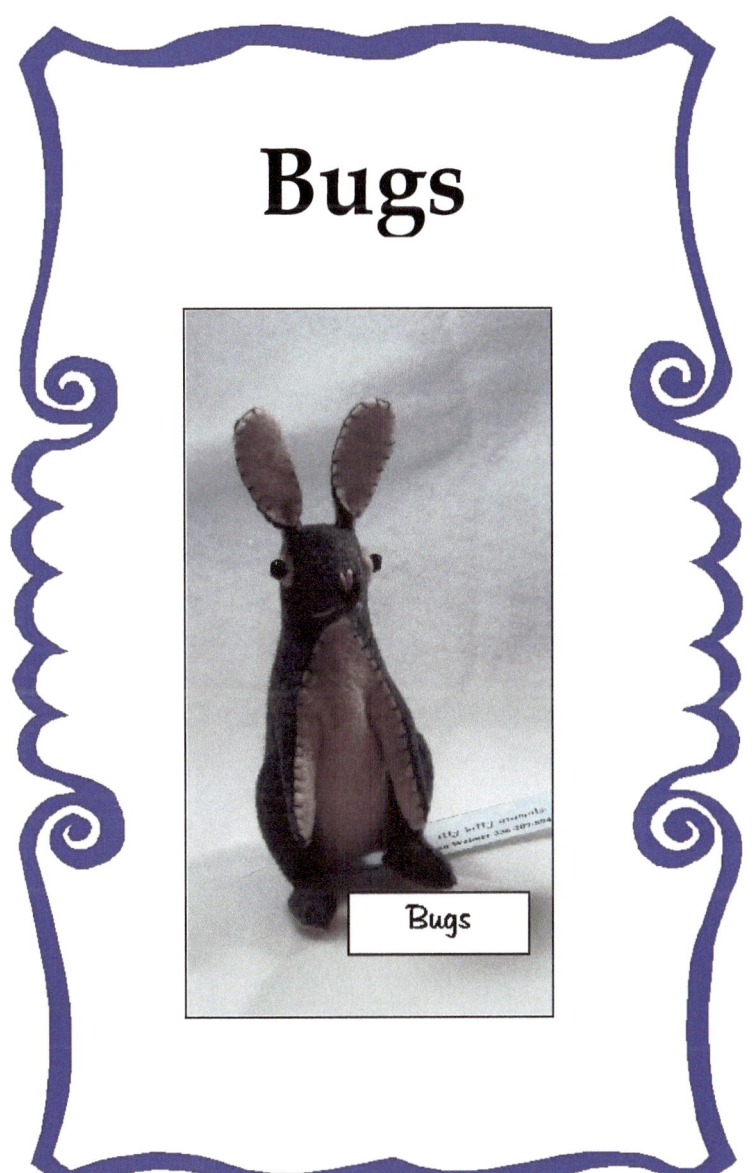

This is Cleopatra. She is a very loving and passionate rabbit. She loves children and elders and anyone in between the ages of 3 – 110. She loves to travel and frequents Egypt and Italy. She has had all her shots; she is spayed; she is housebroken and has a microchip. She is a good judge of character and can see that you are the right person for her. She makes a good sleeping companion and would be useful as a watch rabbit. Will you take Cleopatra home with you?

Cleopatra

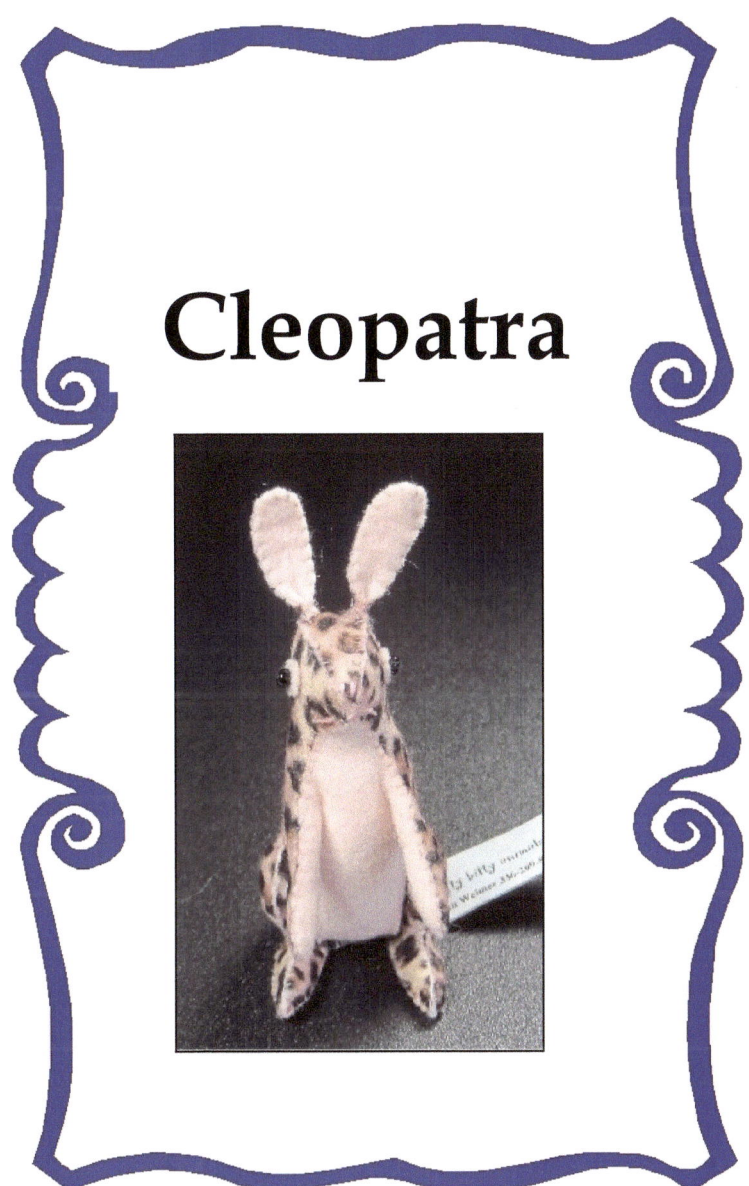

Ginger is girabbit. She is a rabbit in a giraffe's skin. She is very proud of being different. Sometimes other rabbits (and even people) make fun of her and try to bully her because of her strange coat. But Ginger is very even-tempered and endures all the teasing while slowly munching on a carrot. She has had all her shots, is housebroken, has been spayed, and even has a microchip. She loves gardens and wants to become a horticulturist. Is Ginger the right pet for you? Loyalty is her most outstanding virtue.

Ginger

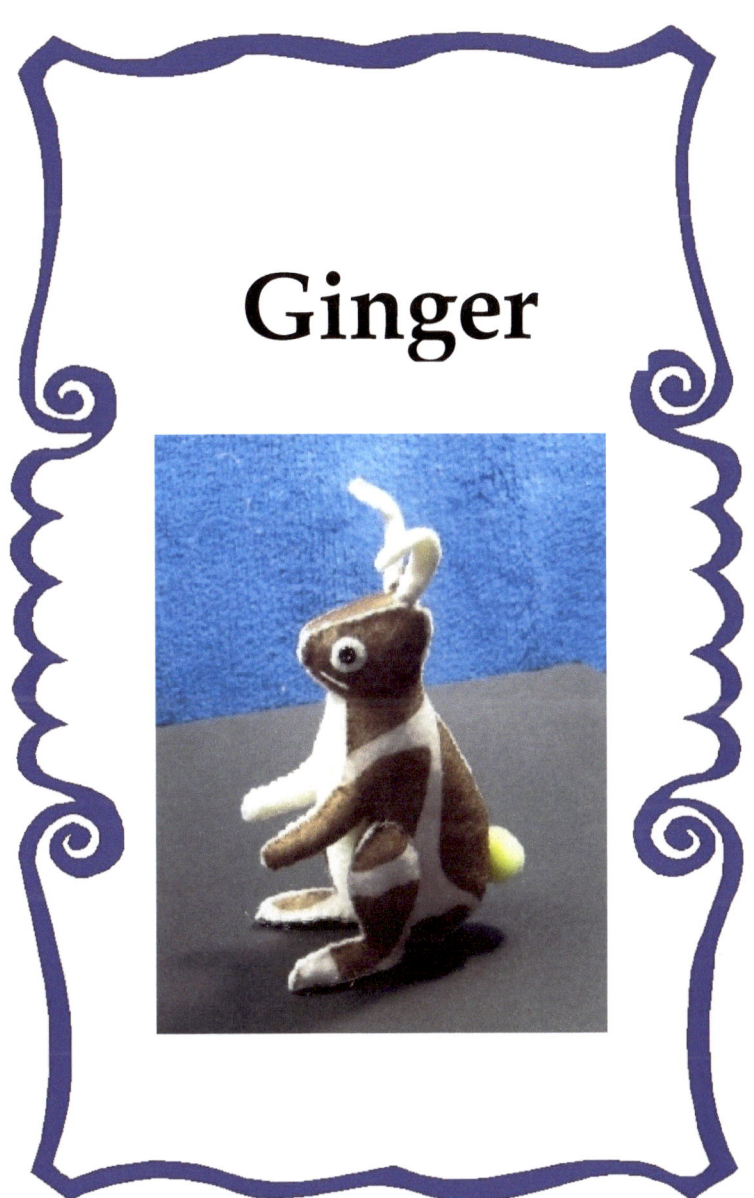

This is Savoy. He is a party rabbit! He loves wearing outlandish clothing and is always ready for a good time. He loves all kinds of snacks especially carrots, celery, and broccoli. He has had all his shots; he is neutered; he is housebroken and has a microchip. Savoy will always dance when you play beach music. He is an all-around genuine good rabbit who will be a loving companion for anyone who loves to have a good time. He will entertain your guests while you work in the kitchen. Is Savoy your kind of rabbit?

Savoy

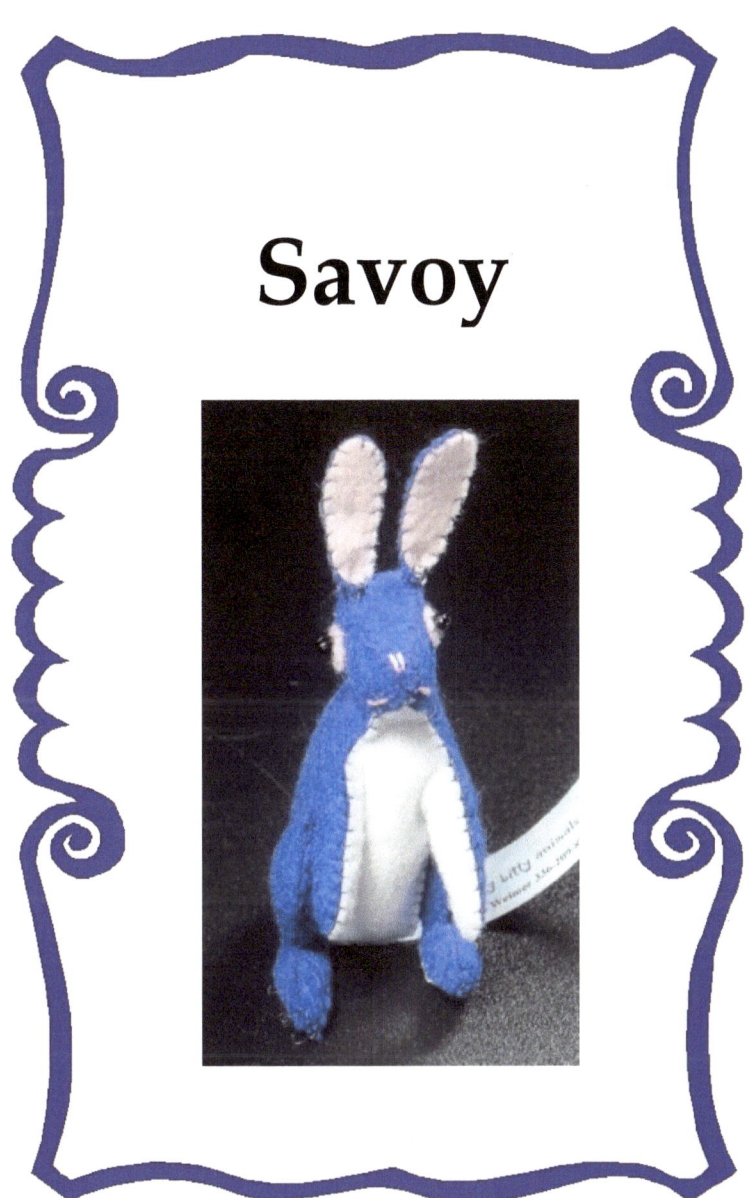

Lime-A-Rita was found in Mexico City doing a Mexican Hat Dance for the few coins people would throw at her. Her lime green coat inspired the name we gave her. She is very talented and wants to become a ballet dancer. She has all her shots, is housebroken and is spayed. Lime-A-Rita can be very temperamental at times but is very gregarious and loves to socialize. Her favorite drink: Lime-A-Rita, of course! Can you provide that atmosphere that will help her realize her dream? She needs lots of encouragement and understanding. Is she right for you?

Lime-a-Rita

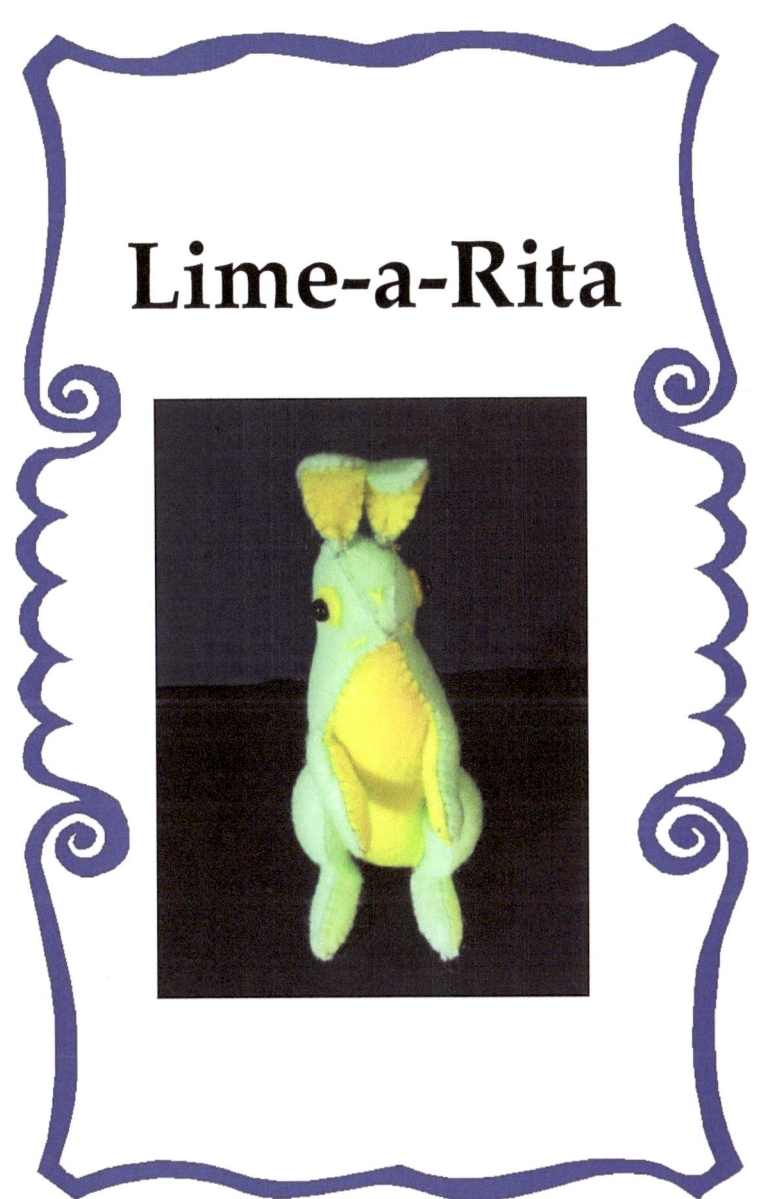

Velveteen is named after the rabbit in the book *The Velveteen Rabbit*. The nursery magic fairy made him REAL. He is a very loyal rabbit and loves to play and make tunnels. Little children hold a special spot in his tender heart. He learned a lot of life's lessons from the Skin Horse and how your relationship with others grows with companionship and love. Velveteen is a child advocate and works hard to support activities and groups that enrich children's lives. Are children special to you? Did you have that special toy when you were young? Then Velveteen is the pet for you.

Velveteen

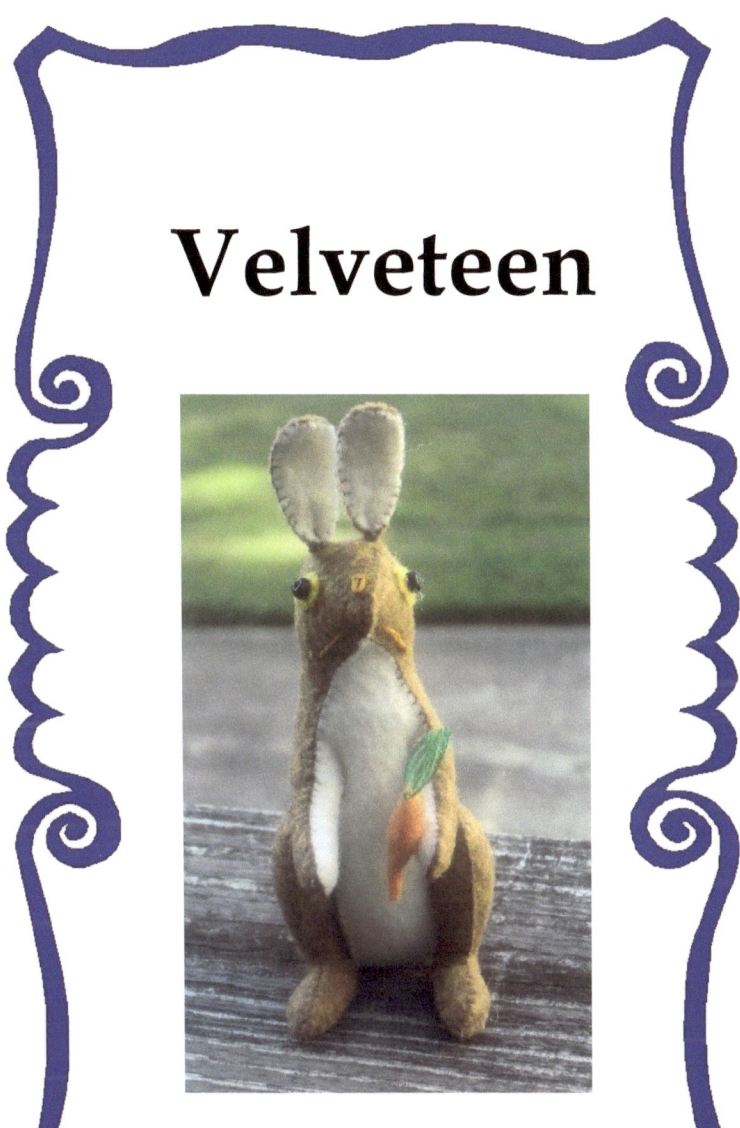

Clover was found in a field of clover in Indiana. During her rehabilitation period we discovered that she was a good cook. Her specialties are clover pie, clover pancakes, clover pizza, clover burrito, and beef & clover stew. She was so talented that she started her very own Clover Cooking School and many famous chefs signed up for training. She loves movies, bowling, and attending craft fairs. She has been housebroken, has all her shots, and even has a microchip! Do you have a special place in your heart for Clover? She is very talented but down to earth

Clover

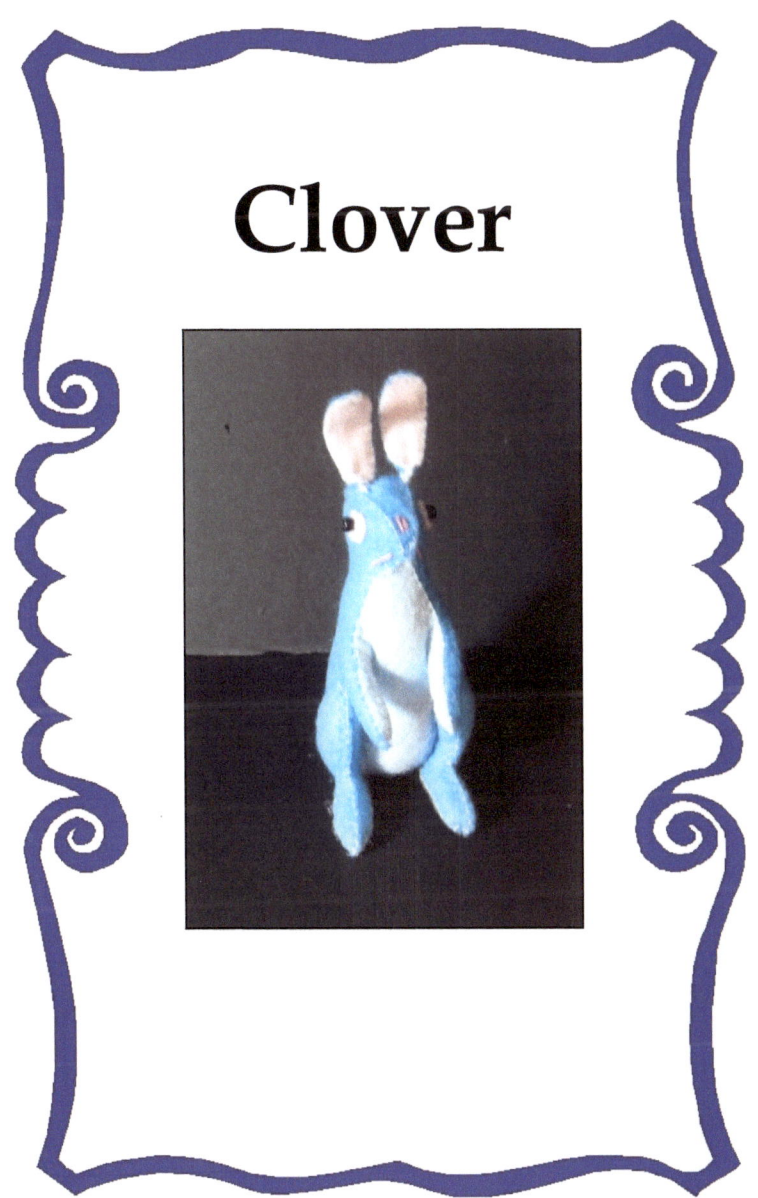

Fluffy is a Halloween rabbit. He owns a haunted house in the Woods of Terror. His main goal is to scare you so that it will last a whole year until next Halloween. He has spiders, mice, rats and ferrets working for him to make your visit to his house as unpleasant as it can be. There is a surprise around every corner, and not all of them are living. He wants to invite you to his house for dinner. Are you brave enough to go? Never know what he might be cooking! If you adopt Fluffy, you will be the envy of all of your friends who appreciate a good scare.

Fluffy

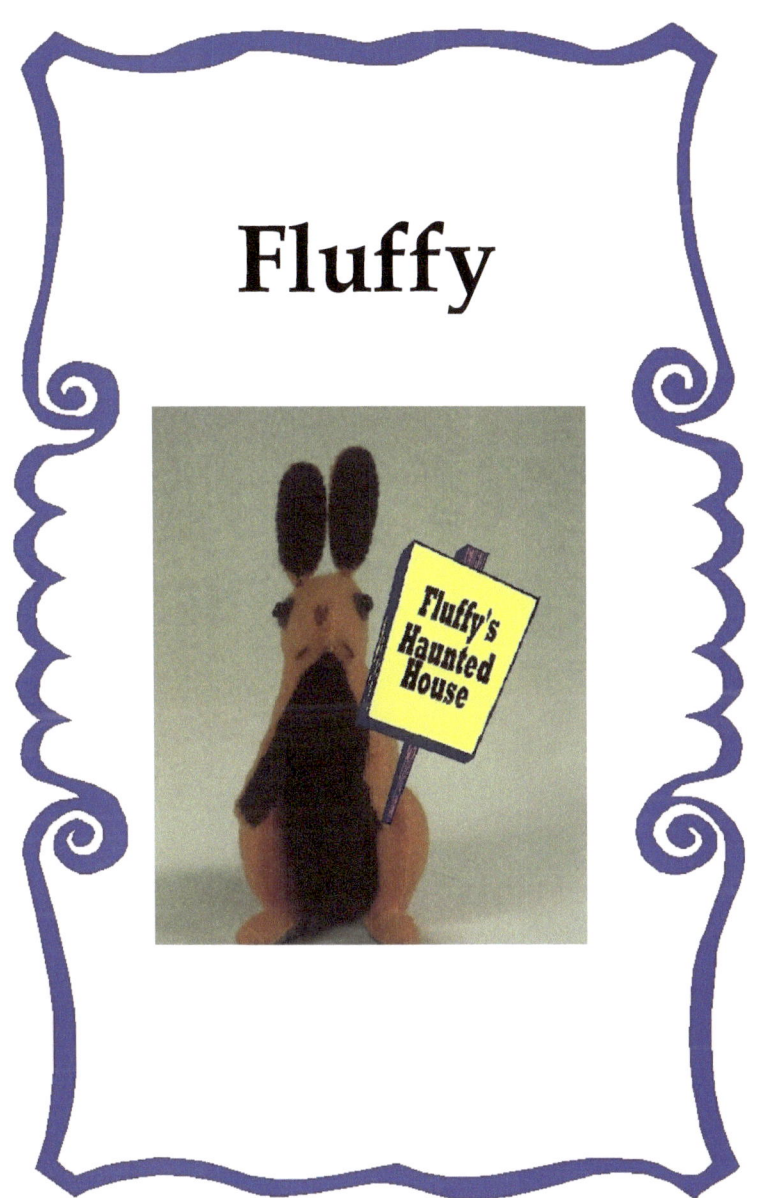

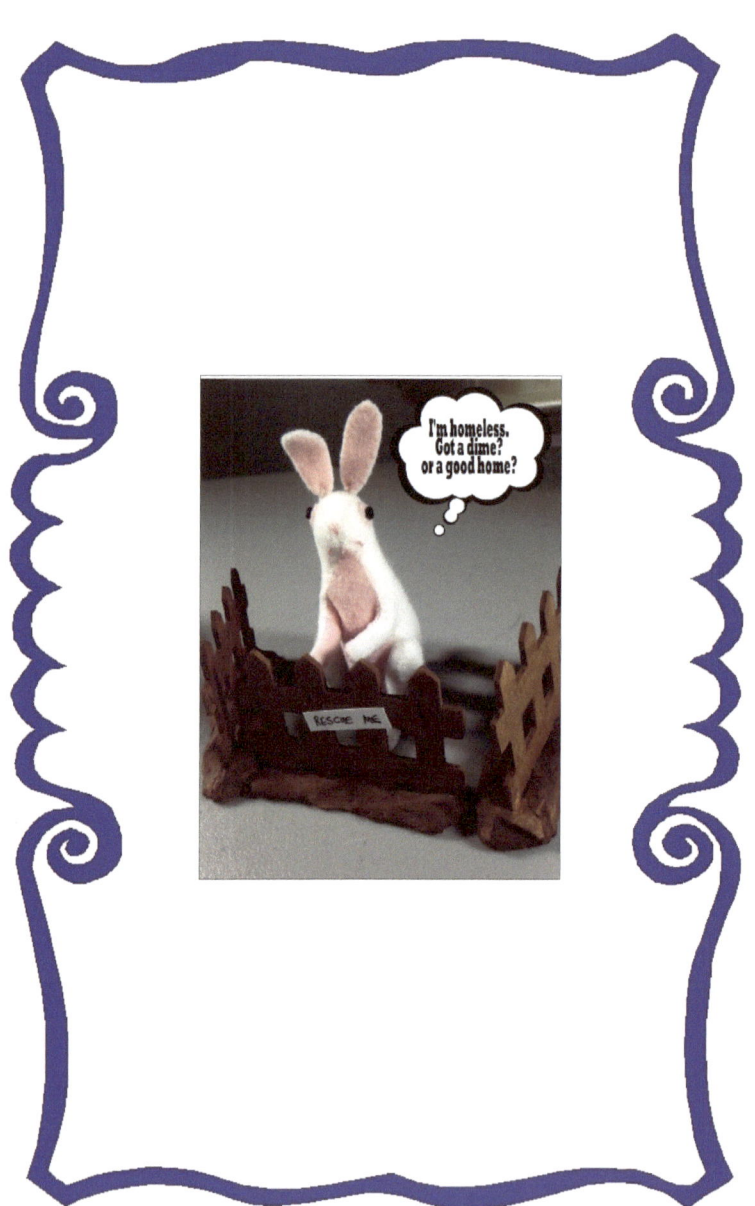

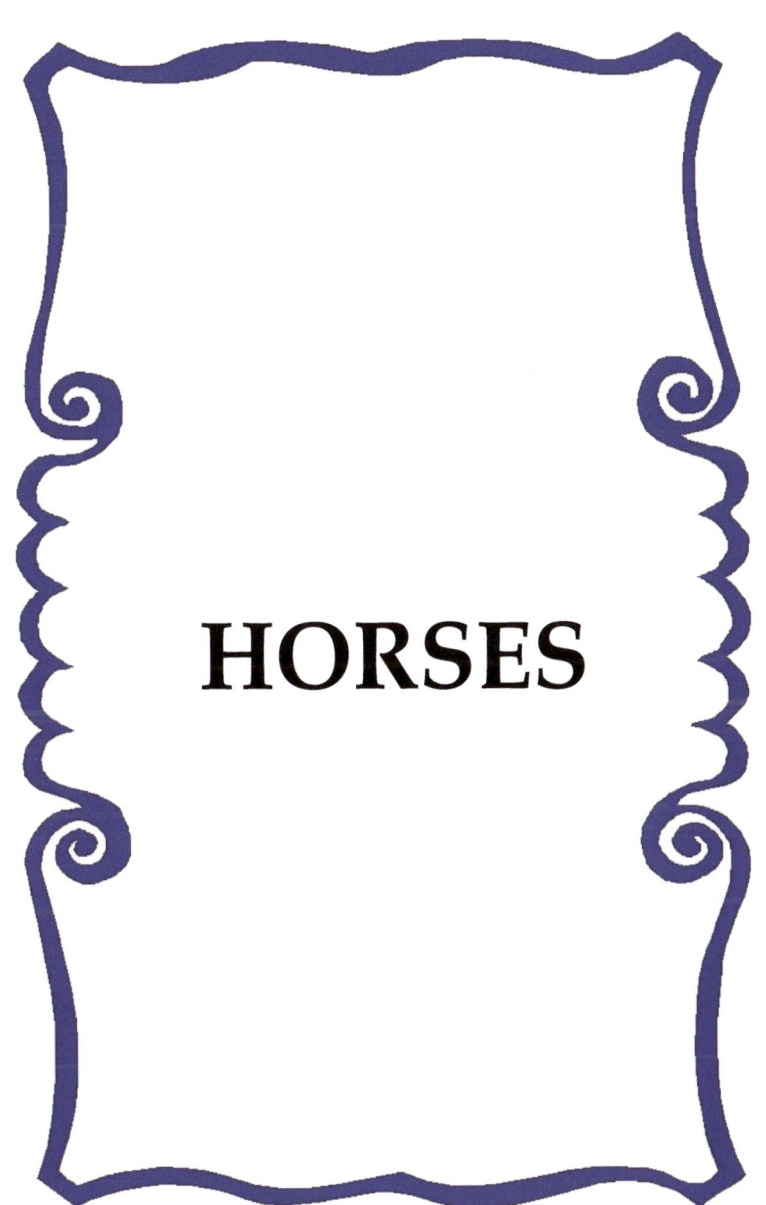

HORSES

Old Paint is a cancer survivor. As she watched the chemotherapy drugs drip into her bloodstream, she was tenacious in her will to survive. A large, gray cloud overshadowed her: "Will this do it?" "I will fight this." "My life is not over, and I have a lot more to give of myself." She dealt with the annoyances of losing her mane and tail hair. Her hooves became cracked and snagged on everything. It was worth it! The day she heard: "You are cancer free!" she went to the tattoo parlor and got a tie-die tattoo.

Old Paint

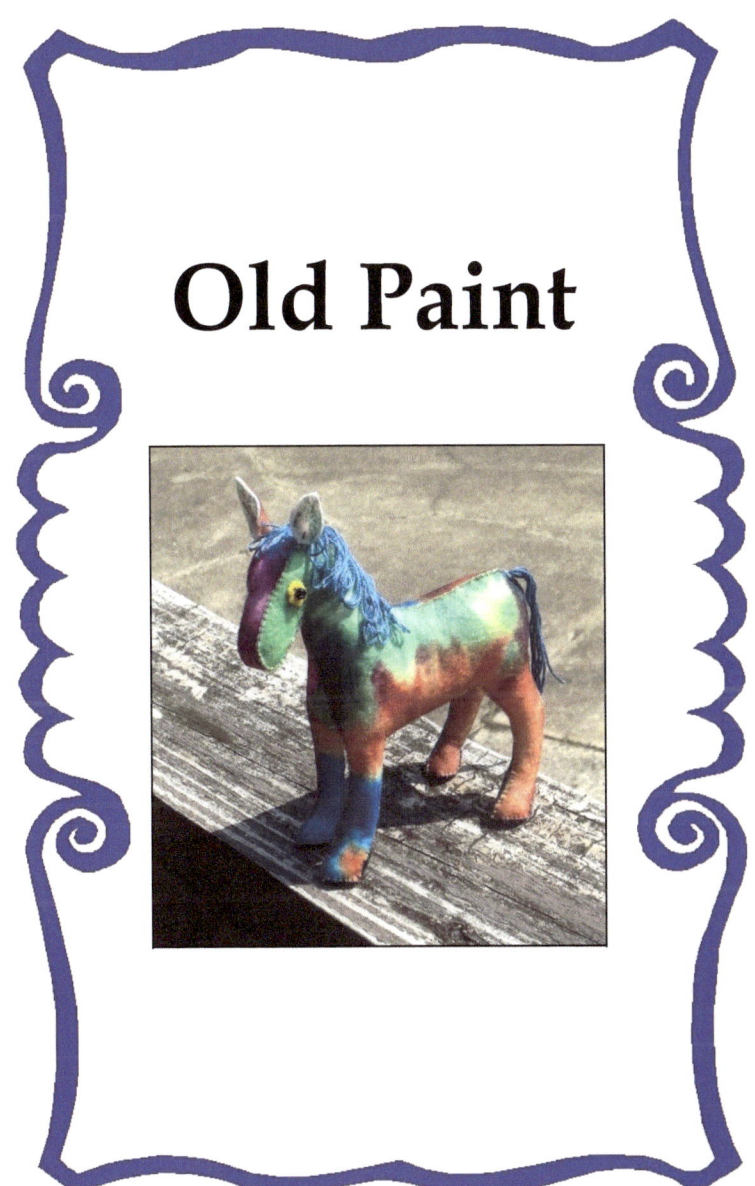

Knight's Mare is a trained nightmare chaser. She uses techniques that she learned at the Ghostbuster Training Center. While you sleep, Knight's Mare will be eliminating your darkest, secret fears and bugaboos. You can rest easy with this horse by your bedside. It will not matter what kind of mattress you are sleeping on or even if you are in a sleeping bag, Knight's Mare has a keen eye for fictional and real hazards. She is not a talisman, an object of worship, or an angel. Knight's Mare is your squeegee pal. She is housebroken, has all her shots, and even had a microchip! Consider adopting her as your "squeegee pal."

Knight's Mare

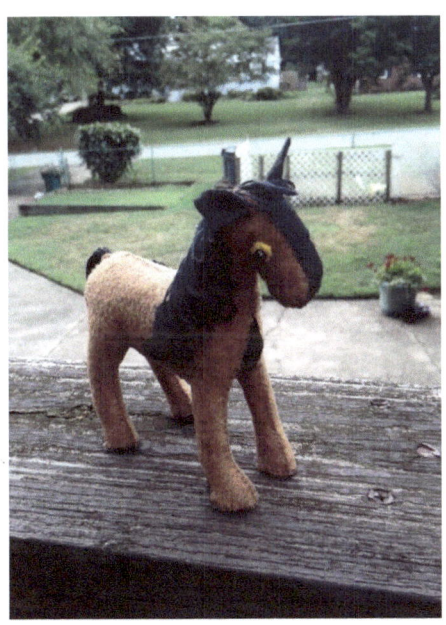

Bean was found in a field of pinto beans. Not knowing the difference between a pinto horse and a pinto bean, he readily adapted to his name, Bean. You can tell Bean any of your secrets because he doesn't speak English. He speaks a perfectly fluent version of Bean. So you are going to have a communication problem, but he is such a charmer you will not even notice this language barrier problem. He loves cuddling, petting, whispering sweet nothings in his ear and any expression of genuine affection. Check out the nearest pinto bean field to see if you can get a glimpse of him. If you find him, take him home with you!

Bean

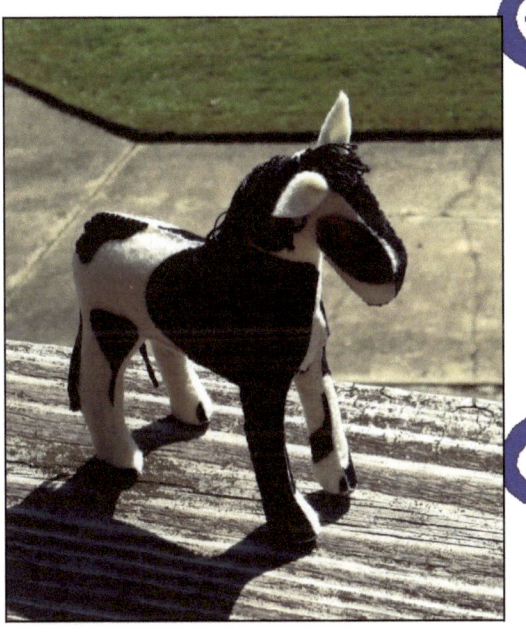

Lightning can achieve 0 – 60 in 30 seconds! Now that's fast! This is no trail riding pony. This pony needs the wide open spaces. Enjoy the thrill of the wind blowing through your hair as you ride the rolling hills of the prairie. After a long, hard ride, Lightning heads to the Oat Barn, his favorite hangout place. There YOU can enjoy a glass of cold, sparkling, bubbly grape juice! No processed food at the Oat Barn. If you are into speed, and grape juice, then Lightning is the pony for you.

Lightning

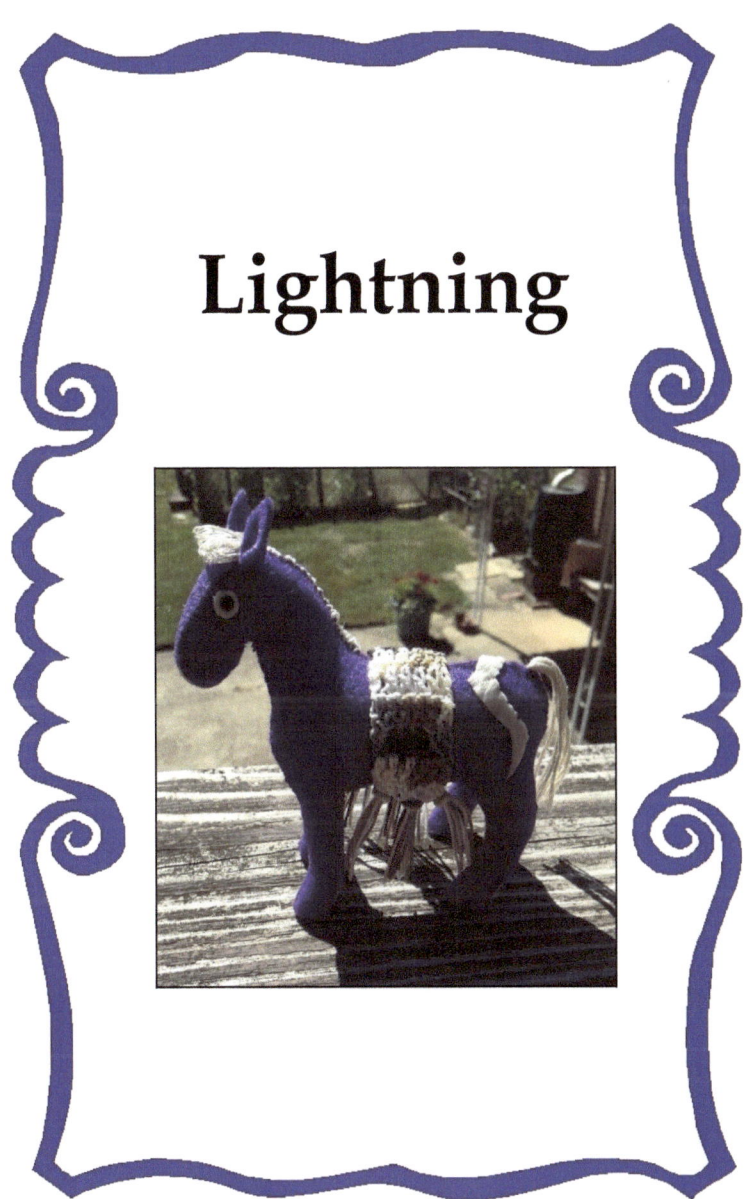

Widow Maker: Ladies, look out! This horse will steal your man away. Widow Maker will blind-side your husband into thinking he is madly in love with this horse and you will be left out in the cold. Do not consider giving this horse to your boyfriend, husband, or significant other. What you might want to do is give it to a man you don't ever want to see again. He will think he has the best horse on earth and will ride off into the sunset, never to be seen again! Beware of the Widow Maker.

Widow Maker

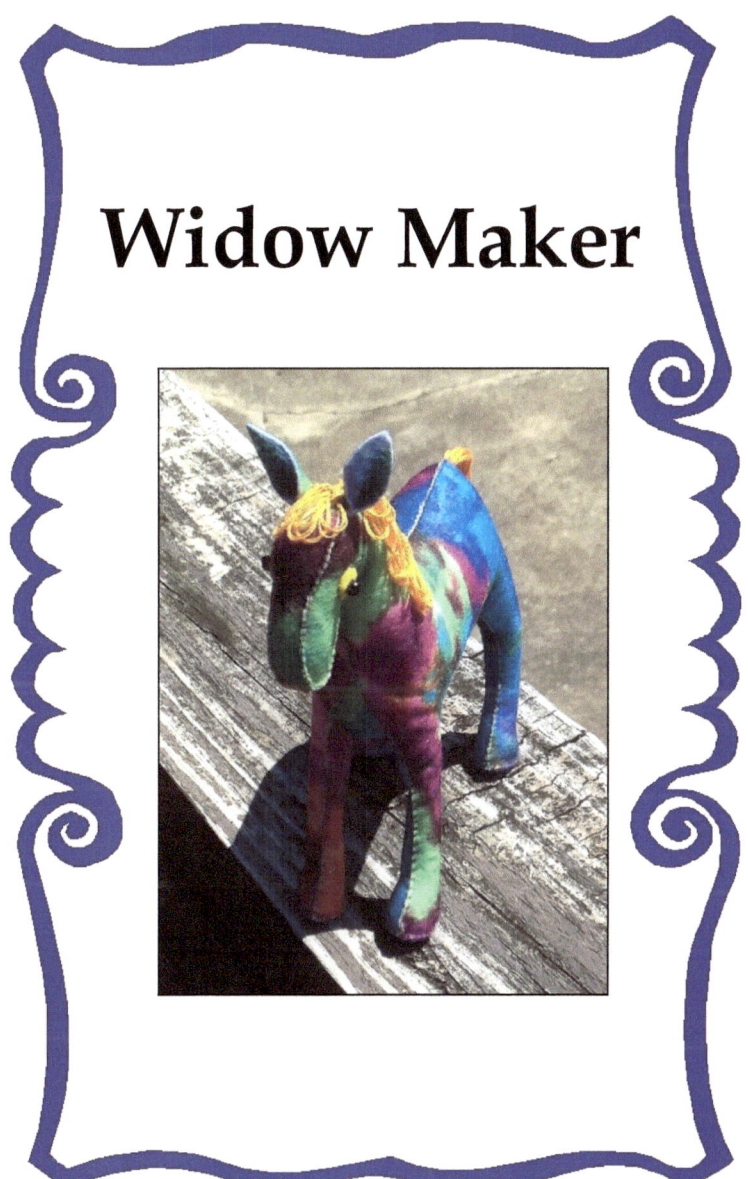

Meet CREDIT CARD. You will see her driving around town in her all-white Kia Soul. You will see her at Friendly Shopping Center and at Four Seasons Mall. She loves to frequent Macys, Belk's, J.C. Penney, Kohl's and the Cheesecake Factory. Exxon is the only kind of gas she allows in her Kia Soul. She is a woman of impeccable taste, charm, and grace. Her house is immaculate and fit for a Presidential fund raiser. She moves with elegance through high society but manages to provide a few pennies for the Food Bank. She has one bad habit: This horse likes to charge!

Credit Card

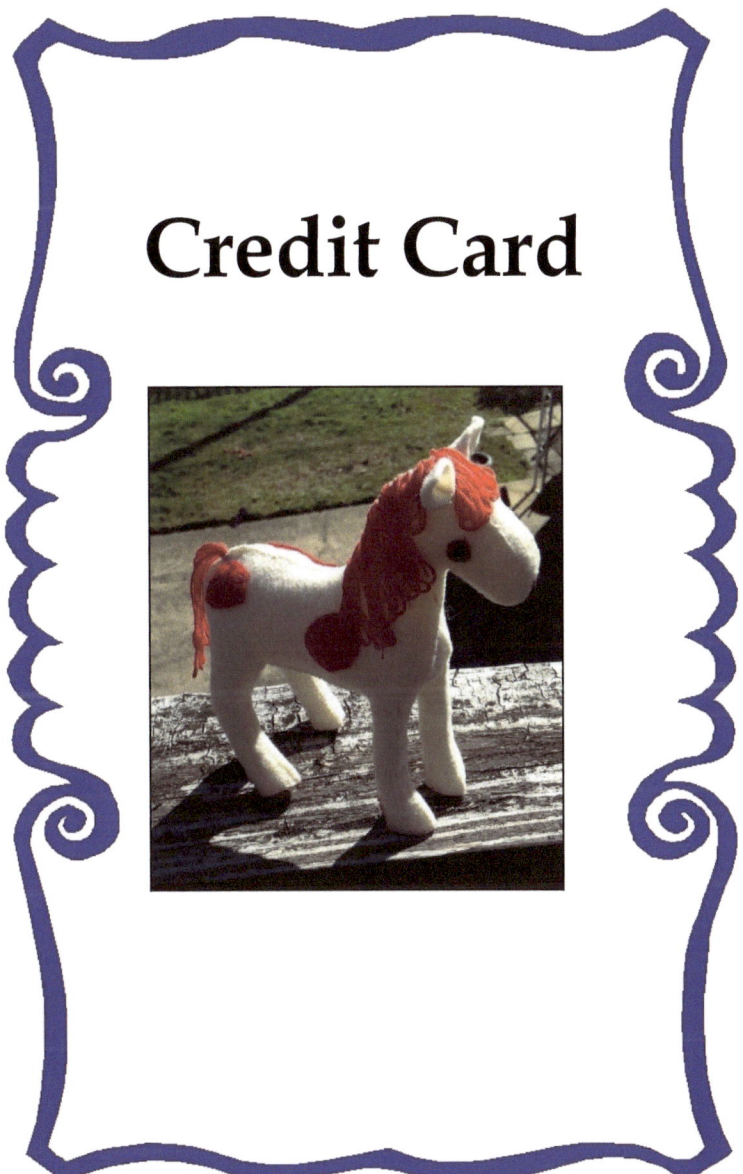

Old Master is the owner of a quality craft Brewing Factory. He pursued the finest ingredients to produce a mellow, transparent, foamy beer that pleases the palates of millions. He knows he is not a Clydesdale, but strives to provide the finest beer at American football stadiums. Old Master's finest beer is a favorite at beer tasting events and has won many awards. Are you the ultimate beer taster? Can you settle for a horse that is less than a Clydesdale? Are you into craft beer and beer tasting? Then Old Master will be the perfect companion for you.

Old Master

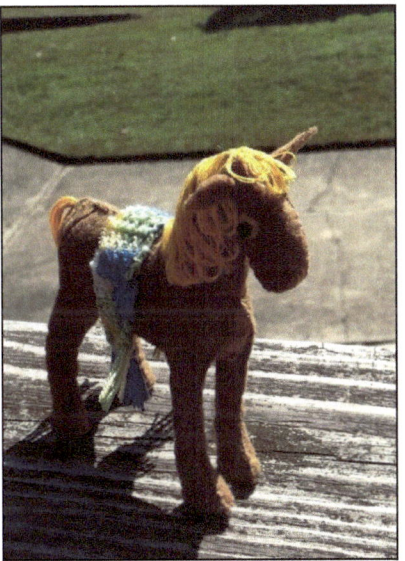

Huu, huu, huu. You're the one that I love! BILLIE JEAN, you are my beauty queen! She can turn on a dime, and she's all mine! She can prance; she can dance; she can keep you entranced. She will blow you away with her fancy dance moves – graceful, elegant, lithe, and smooth. When you see her magnificent form clear the hurdles then you are convinced: "That horse is so fine! Billie Jean, you are mine!" My stables are your kingdom. Huu, huu, huu. You're the one that I love. Huu, huu, huu. You're the one that I love. Looking for that special horse in your life? Itty Bitty Animals transformed BILLIE JEAN from a street horse to a beauty queen. She is looking for her forever home. Are you open to some special loving from BILLIE JEAN?

Billie Jean

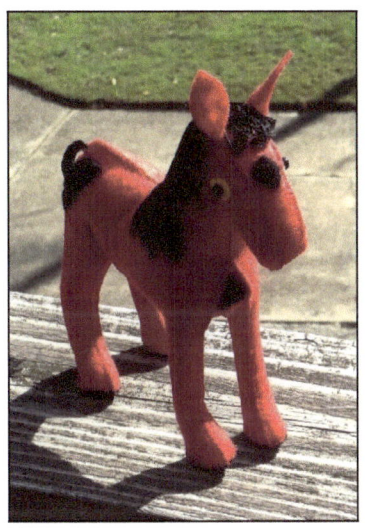

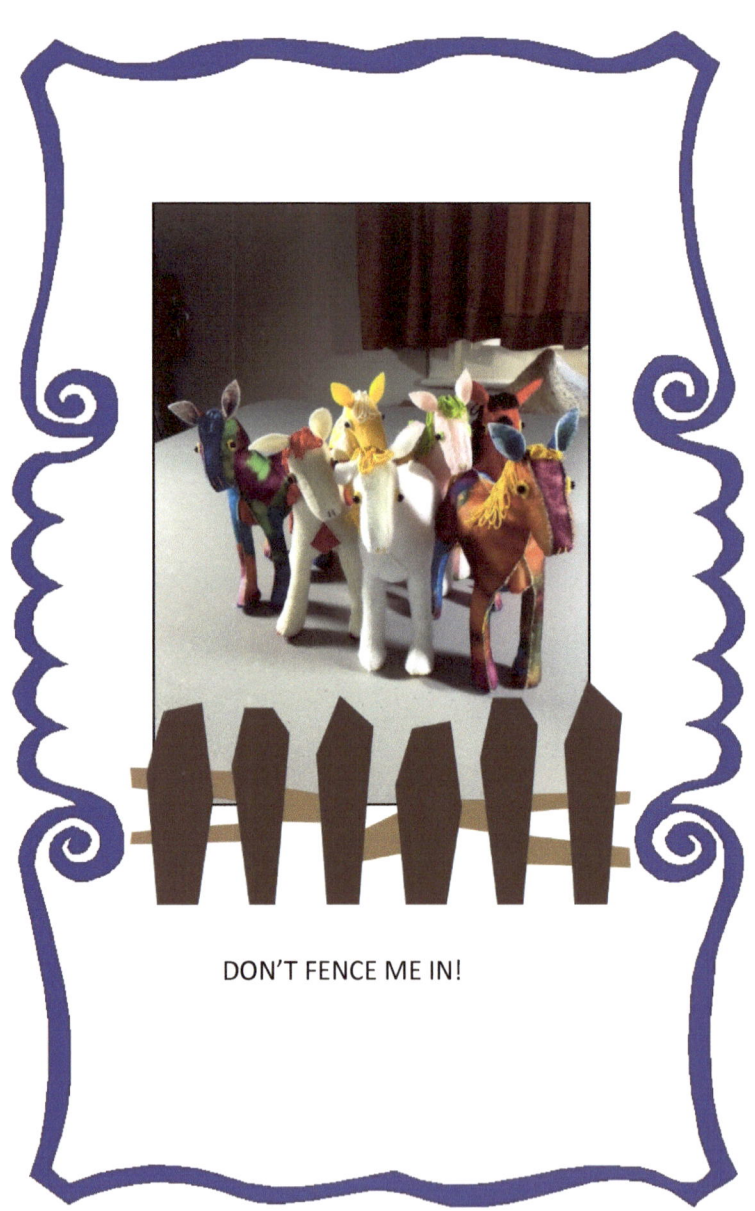

DON'T FENCE ME IN!

www.ingramcontent.com/pod-product-compliance
Lightning Source LLC
Chambersburg PA
CBHW040223220526
45473CB00001B/100